THE
Eddie Bauer
GUIDE TO
CROSS-COUNTRY
SKIING

THE
Eddie Bauer
GUIDE TO
CROSS-COUNTRY
SKIING

ARCHIE SATTERFIELD
EDDIE BAUER

ILLUSTRATIONS BY TED RAND

ADDISON-WESLEY PUBLISHING COMPANY
READING, MASSACHUSETTS • MENLO PARK, CALIFORNIA
LONDON • AMSTERDAM • DON MILLS, ONTARIO • SYDNEY

Library of Congress Cataloging in Publication Data

Satterfield, Archie.
  The Eddie Bauer guide to cross-country skiing.

  Includes index.
  1. Cross-country skiing. 2. Cross-country skiing—Equipment and supplies.
3. Cross-country skiing—United States.
I. Bauer, Eddie, II. Title.
GV855.3.S27 1983   796.93   83-11909
ISBN 0-201-07774-4
ISBN 0-201-07775-2 (pbk.)

Cover photograph by David Barnes,
© 1983 Aperture Photo Bank
Cover design by Val Paul Taylor
Text design by Val Paul Taylor
Production supervised by B & W Hutchinsons, Inc.,
Orleans, MA
Set in 10-point Lubalin by Crane Typesetting
Service, Inc., Barnstable, MA

ISBN 0-201-07774-4 (H)
ISBN 0-201-07775-2 (P)
ABCDEFGHIJ-DO-86543

First printing, September 1983

THE EDDIE BAUER OUTDOOR LIBRARY

Eddie Bauer has been serving the needs of outdoor enthusiasts for three generations. Since 1920, we have been dedicated to developing, testing, and manufacturing the finest in apparel and gear for outdoor adventures. Our aim has always been to make outdoor adventures more enjoyable.

Now, over sixty years after we began, we are answering the needs of another generation of outdoor activists. Eddie Bauer Outdoor Guides like this one on Cross-Country Skiing will help newcomers get started. Others will contain up-to-date, tested information to make your outdoor excursions safe, warm, dry, and comfortable.

CONTENTS

ACKNOWLEDGMENTS

Books of this nature are always a team effort, and many individuals and companies have been helpful in doing research, reading drafts of the manuscript, and bringing additional material to my attention.

Several members of the Eddie Bauer, Inc., staff have devoted many hours to this book. These include Abbie Anderson, Jim Wheat, Ken Wherry, Bob Murphy, Marilyn Siehl, and Cort Green, who recently retired from the staff.

Information on new developments in camping equipment came from the literature from Eddie Bauer, Inc., suppliers and a selection of books, pamphlets, and product-information releases from them.

Cross-country skiing and winter camping is a relatively new sport for most Americans, and as a result several excellent books have been written recently about them. For information on various aspects of winter recreation, I have relied on these books for further information:

Cross-Country Ski Gear by Michael Brady. Seattle: The Mountaineers, 1979.

The Cross-Country Ski Book by John Caldwell. Brattleboro, Vermont: The Stephen Green Press, 1981.

Winter Camping by Bob Cary. Brattleboro, Vermont: The Stephen Greene Press, 1979.

Mountaineering: The Freedom of the Hills by The Climbing Committee of The Mountaineers, ed. Peggy Ferber. Seattle: The Mountaineers, 1960, 1967, 1974.

Cross-Country Skiing by Ned Gillette. Seattle: The Mountaineers, 1979.

Snow by Ruth Kirk. New York: William Morrow & Co., 1978.

Backpacking, One Step at a Time by Harvey Manning. Seattle: Recreational Equipment, Inc., 1972.

Wintering by Russ Mohney. Harrisburg, Pennsylvania: Stackpole Books, 1976.

Competing in Cross-Country Skiing by B.H. Nilsson, trans. Maxine Hobson. New York: Sterling Publishing, 1979.

The L.L. Bean Guide to the Outdoors by Bill Riviere. New York: Random House, 1981.

Movin' On by Harry Roberts. Boston: Stone Wall Press, 1977.

The Wilderness Route Finder by Calvin Rutstrum. New York: Collier Books, 1967.

Wilderness Skiing by Lito Tejada-Flores and Allen Steck. San Francisco: Sierra Club Books, 1972.

Ski Camping by Ron Watters. San Francisco: Chronicle Books, 1979.

Medicine For Mountaineering by James A. Wilkerson, M.D. Seattle: The Mountaineers, 1975.

Cross-Country Ski Routes by Richard Wright and Rochelle Wright. Lynnwood, Washington: Signpost Books, 1978.

Periodicals

Cross Country Skier, West River Road, Brattleboro, Vermont.

Ski X-C, One Park Avenue, New York.

—Archie Satterfield

FOREWORD

While serving my seven-year apprenticeship in the outfitting business, from 1913 until 1920 at Piper & Taft in Seattle, I saw that snow sport inventories and annual sales were practically nil; one dozen pairs of two-groove ash skis made by Strand or Lund, and perhaps several dozen pairs of snowshoes were about the extent of that business. The stores seemed content to merely meet consumer demands rather than create new forms of recreation. However, I felt that there were many opportunities in outdoor recreation during the winter and early spring months that weren't being explored.

It was during the winter of 1920–21 that my eyes were opened to the opportunity in recreational skiing. This came about during an outing with The Mountaineers of Seattle, a fine climbing and hiking club that went on numerous outings each year. Two of my friends, who were members of the club, had hunted with me in the fall of 1921 and asked if I would go along as "bull cook." Bull cooks do all the dirty work: peel the spuds, scrub the pots and pans, carry the wood and water. But I was happy to join them, since I was self-employed with spare time to be away from my first store, and I had never been on Mt. Rainier during the winter.

We had our work cut out for us, because there were 150 or more members. Fortunately, all the food except the meat and produce had been shipped to Paradise Inn before the outing, so we didn't have to carry everything in with us. We took the train from Seattle to Ashford and then hiked in to Longmire on snowshoes over a trail that had already been broken by the club members.

We spent that night at Longmire, and the next morning we three hired hands left early to get to Paradise Inn ahead of the group and have the first meal ready when they arrived. It was a hard trip, as each of us was carrying around 100 pounds of fresh meat and produce, so we took turns breaking trail on the five-mile hike to the inn. But it was also a beautiful trip, because all the evergreens were heavily laden with snow and the waterfalls were completely frozen over.

It was a great outing. The Mountaineers all pitched in on the chores, such as house cleaning, dishwashing, waiting on tables, and providing entertainment.

One of the members brought along a pair of two-groove cross-country skis, and everyone in the group took turns trying them out, enjoying them immensely.

After this outing, I decided to work towards developing a cross-country ski business in the Pacific Northwest as a much-needed form of outdoor winter recreation. I already had some experience with skis through my friendship with trappers from the eastern Cascade Mountains to the Rockies, who worked traplines of up to 100 miles using homemade skis, waxes, and harnesses. The commercial skis available in North America were pretty primitive by foreign standards, but this was not so with some of the homemade varieties.

The trappers, who made excellent skis, would look for a birch tree growing on a hillside with a bend near the butt that provided a permanent tip bend, like a shovel. A seven- or eight-foot section was carefully cut, peeled, and split, and then air-dried under cover.

These cured blanks were then carefully shaped, quite wide by today's standards, and in suitable lengths for the person who would use them.

Then matched pairs were steam-cambered and finished, then moisture-proofed. Waxes were made from various formulas: natural resins, paraffin, perhaps animal and fish oils and fats. The bottom surface, or base, was paraffin-impregnated with old-fashioned flatirons, which served the purpose very well.

My first stores were too small to sell ski products, but I kept an eye on the potential market and went out with friends on cross-country trips occasionally.

When I opened my third store, in 1928, we were the first to stock and promote high-quality Norwegian, German, and Swiss imported skis. We designed and sold ski clothing, and as a result many of our customers took up the sport.

Then in 1933, we opened our fourth store, Seattle's largest, and went all-out to promote skiing. We employed experts from Norway, such as Roy Nerland, Olaf Ulland, and several others who were champions at jumping, downhill, slalom, and cross-country. Others, such as Ome Daiber, Scott Osborn, and Hans Grage, soon joined us. Our business grew rapidly, and we installed complete facilities in service, repair, and light manufacturing. Clubs were formed, lodges were built, roads were maintained the year-round, and new resorts were planned.

By 1938, we had four stores, all featuring ski products. Roy Nerland was elected president of the Seattle Ski Club, and Ome Daiber founded mountain rescue teams that still carry on his tradition.

By then, a new industry was well under way, and the combined efforts of people and businesses with vision throughout America and Canada have given us the leadership in the industry we enjoy today.

—Eddie Bauer

A NOTE ON STYLE

The accepted abbreviation for cross-country skiing is simply x-c skiing, and it will be used frequently throughout the book.

Although the United States is committed to switching over to the metric system in the near future, very few children and even fewer adults have made the mental switch. Consequently, when discussing ski lengths, course lengths, and other terms which have traditionally been used in skiing circles, the metric system will be followed. But English units will be used for common measurements, such as individual height and weight.

PART I
THE JOYS OF CROSS-COUNTRY SKIING

CHAPTER 1

INTRODUCTION

One of life's greatest pleasures is to wake early on a winter's morning in a mountain cabin, knowing that the rest of your companions are still asleep. The fire in the woodstove has been out for hours, and the insides of the windows are coated with frost. You know without looking that the water in the teakettle on the stove has a thin sheet of ice on it. You suspect that some of your companions are awake, too, but they are going to play a waiting game with you, hoping you will get up first and start the fire.

You aren't close enough to the stove to reach it without leaving your sleeping bag, so you lie there, plotting your moves so you can jump out of the bag, shake the ashes off the grate, put in dry tinder and kindling, adjust the damper, and light the fire, all without wasting a motion or a moment. Then you dive back into the sleeping bag to wait for the warm.

When the cabin is toasty and your sleeping bag is almost too warm, you unzip it, convinced there is not a more comfortable place on earth than in this cabin, heated by a woodstove, with snow up on the roof and silence outside in the forest. You lie there a few more minutes, savoring these thoughts, before crawling out again with your toes involuntarily curling against the frigid floor.

You dress and step outside, knowing that those who have been pretending sleep will shout in outrage when you open the door and let the frigid air into the cabin. Once you are outside, you are immediately struck by the deep, everlasting silence and beauty of the winter landscape: icicles, hanging from the cabin roof; the sun, compensating for its lack of heat with a glare that makes your eyes water; a suggestion of a breeze, stirring the powdery snow on the porch and sending glistening crystals flying through the air; yesterday's footprints, now cakes of ice on the porch; and ski tracks leading off into the woods— a promise.

You hurry back into the cabin, rouse your companions with cheerful insults, begin breakfast, and start assembling your equipment for another day of traveling through the white forest on your skis.

Similar scenarios are followed every day throughout the winter somewhere in North America, most often in centrally heated lodges, hotels, and condominium complexes in the forests. Although the majority of cross-country skiers enjoy their sport with this sort of comfort, still an increasing number of skiers are hikers and backpackers during the summer months who strike out on their own into the white wilderness packing tents, stoves, and food on their backs or in small sleds (**pulkas**) they tow along behind them. With today's ultralight and compact camping equipment, the thought of camping in the snow no longer conjures up visions of packing 100 pounds or more of equipment to insure comfort. Tents and clothing for sub-zero weather have little more weight and bulk than do spring and fall-rated equipment.

The number of winter campers is growing steadily, although there are still many who think of the first frost as the time of year to put away their out-door gear until the next Memorial Day and settle instead for the specialized downhill skiing. Many still think of winter outdoor recreation in terms of survival situations when winter is hardly more dangerous than summer. The dangers are only different.

According to a 1979 survey by A. C. Nielsen, more than 14 million Americans participated in snow skiing, which was an increase of 40 percent over the survey taken in 1976. The 1979 survey showed that 72 percent of those polled were Alpine (downhill) skiers, and 19 percent were Nordic (cross-country) skiers. The remaining nine percent enjoyed both downhill and cross-country skiing.

More recent figures aren't available yet, but it is known that x-c skiing has taken a quantum leap in popularity over the past few years. One indication of this growth is that more than 600 touring centers are listed across North America, but only one in six of them operates in conjunction with a downhill ski area.

In a sense, x-c skiing has taken up where hiking and backpacking leave off when the snow falls. And in most cases, skiing has replaced snowshoeing as a form of recreation because ski equipment has been steadily improved. Such a wide variety of equipment has been developed that x-c skis can be found for almost any requirement. And each season brings even more improvements, making it easier and easier for us to enjoy the winter.

Although the example has been overworked for years, the case of the Eskimos in the Arctic is worth repeating. These people are so well-adapted to winter that they look forward to its return for many reasons. The hordes of mosquitoes, flies, and other insects leave with summer; also, winter is cleaner than summer because nothing decays. Travel is much simpler in the winter because snow and ice make a much better surface than do ground and water. It is easier to dress for winter than summer because you can keep putting on clothing to protect yourself against the cold, but you can remove only so much clothing to find relief from the heat. Also, you can build fires for warmth and add covers at night, but you can't do much to find comfort in extreme heat, especially on a hot, still night.

Cross-country skiing has soared in popularity over the last few decades, due in part to the improved equipment that has been available only since the 1940s. This new technology in clothing and shelter was developed during the World War II era. The goose-down sleeping bags and clothing developed by Eddie Bauer for the U.S. Army Air Corps and other branches of the service quickly found a civilian market for civilian uses, enabling people to enjoy the winter as never before.

Still another contributing factor to the growth of x-c skiing has been the phenomenal growth of downhill skiing. Many x-c skiers are former downhill skiers who wanted an alternative to the crowded slopes and increasingly expensive equipment and lift tickets. Cross-country skiing provides this alternative, as both the gear and trail fees are less costly. And although x-c ski manufacturers have been gradually closing the gap between x-c and downhill skis, offering more and more versatility, it is doubtful that one pair of skis will ever be perfect for both uses.

If you are a year-round outdoors-man, as most x-c skiers are, you will find that much of your summer equipment can easily be adapted to winter use. The layering system of clothing used in summer camping is just as essential for winter comfort, and except for specialized gear—boots, gloves or mittens, and headgear—much of your summerweight clothing will also serve as part of your winter layering system.

Consequently, you will be able to travel and camp in comfort without having to carry or tow an enormous burden of clothing, bedding, and shelter. The difference in weight between summer and winter camping is less than you would expect, only a matter of a few pounds. This is especially true if you use goose-down sleeping bags and clothing, where the difference in insulation value is measured in ounces rather than pounds.

There are still other factors which recommend x-c skiing, including solitude and freedom of movement. Few downhill skiers venture away from ski lifts and popular slopes in the winter months. But x-c skiers find it much easier to get away from the crowds, rest on their skis, and listen to the silence.

You can camp near a rural road that is busy and dusty in the summer but used only by local residents in the winter. You can also travel across land that you wouldn't consider hiking on in the summer, when it looks so flat and uninteresting without the snow cover. But put on a pair of x-c skis or snowshoes and this same land becomes attractive because you need less effort to travel.

Another advantage is that property owners are more likely to allow winter travelers on skis or snowshoes to use their property than summer backpackers because the potential for

damage is much less when the ground is covered with snow.

The freedom offered by x-c skiing is so great that it can hardly be compared to downhill skiing. You can go virtually anywhere you want on x-c skis; all you need is snow. Cross-country skiers can even go on mountaineering expeditions, sometimes strapping a pair of snowshoes on their packs to help work their way through brush and around boulders.

The lakes where you swam or canoed during the summer make excellent winter training grounds for learning the basic x-c techniques, and the campgrounds along the shores will be virtually deserted during the winter. You can find many downhill ski areas with x-c skiing down the back slopes. And once you're away from the established ski runs, one ride up the chair lift may suffice for an entire day's ski touring before returning to your car in the parking lot.

With the sport's increasing popularity have come a number of year-round resorts that lay out x-c ski tracks and routes and offer instruction and rentals. Some ski areas are truly spectacular, such as one found near Palm Springs, California. There x-c skiers can move from the swimming pools and golf courses of the famous resort town to the ski trails, all in less than an hour. A tramway runs from the valley floor,

where temperatures will be in the 80°s most of the winter, up to the top of the San Jacinto Mountains, where snow lies deep during the entire winter. The 8,000-plus-foot tramway ride is probably the fastest trip between these

NOMENCLATURE

What is cross-country skiing? What makes it different from downhill skiing?

Basically, downhill (Alpine) skiing is simply what it says: The skis, bindings, and boots are designed for you to move in only one direction—down. At best, you can ski across level ground, and with a great deal of effort, you can herringbone your way up a slope. But downhill skis have none of the qualities required for striding across the field and through the forest.

Cross-country (Nordic) skis, boots, and bindings are designed for you to go both uphill and downhill and across flat or rolling ground without slipping backward with every step. Cross-country skis let you walk across the snow with a minimum of effort. A type of wax or pattern built into the ski bottom grips to prevent you from sliding backwards while allowing you to slide forward with little effort.

Although designers are hard at work trying to invent a ski which will serve both downhill and cross-country purposes, the qualities needed for excellence in each type of skiing have made this a difficult—if not impossible—task.

Light-touring: Skiing at established cross-country areas where trails have been laid out for skiers.

Touring: Traveling across untracked areas but not steep, rugged terrain.

Mountain skiing: The most difficult kind of x-c skiing—the wintertime equivalent of expeditions and climbing attempts.

Racing: Skis and boots made for this sport are the lightest available, so the skier doesn't have to worry about breaking trail or using the heavy-duty equipment needed for other types of skiing.

Telemarking: A turning technique that has an interesting history; its "rediscovery" in America has resulted in a whole new approach to x-c skiing. This turn was developed in the 1860s near the town of Telemark, Norway, by a jumper named Sondre Nordheim, who used the deep-knee-bend turn to finish off his jumps. Even though the telemark was only reintroduced to America within the past two decades, it has resulted in such a blending of downhill and x-c techniques that they are almost the same for some skiers. Telemarking skis are stiffer and often have offset steel edges to increase turning ability; they are also lightweight, like x- c skis, and may have waxable or machine-patterned bottoms.

temperature extremes found in America.

While the focus of this book is on the beginner, we hope to help all skiers sort through the many types of ski equipment, which should reduce the frustration they feel upon entering a store and seeing all the equipment on display.

We will also discuss other forms of winter recreation, such as camping, that are available to x-c skiers, along with the knowledge and equipment involved in staying overnight in the snow. We will also discuss winter safety considerations, including avalanche safety, protection against the cold, and basic first-aid measures.

Skiing is a form of recreation in itself. Many people are content to go on day-long ski trips, returning to their lodge or home in the evening. But when x-c skiing is combined with other forms of recreation, it becomes a pleasurable means of wilderness transportation, as well as an alternative to running or jogging for exercise. When it is combined with camping, it becomes a total winter sport of equal value to summer camping and hiking.

Whether you decide to use x-c skiing as a means of getting to wil-

CODE OF ETHICS FOR X-C SKIERS

The following rules have been established by the Federation Internationale de Ski (FIS), the international executive body of ski associations, to help make x-c skiing pleasant for everyone:

Respect for Others

A cross-country skier must ski in such a manner that he does not endanger others.

Choice of Tracks

A skier should ski in the right-hand track when there is more than one packed track.

Respect for Signs

On a trail marked with indicated direction, a skier should proceed only in that direction.

Poles

Keep poles close to the body whenever near another skier.

Keeping the Trails Clear

A skier who stops should leave the track. In case of a fall, the skier should clear the track without delay.

Overtaking

A skier is permitted to overtake and pass another skier on the left or right.

Control of Speed

A cross-country skier should always adapt his speed to his personal ability, to the prevailing terrain and visibility, and to the traffic on the course.

derness campsites or simply as a form of daily exercise, you should be more concerned about your physical fitness than if you're a downhill skier. Cross-country skiing is similar to swimming in that it requires the use of more muscles than jogging or running, bicycle touring, or even backpacking. The new muscles brought into play are those from the waist up. Skiing requires more arm and shoulder strength than running does and is thus a more complete form of exercise. Your cardiovascular system—your circula-

tory system including the heart, blood vessels, and lungs—will get a complete workout when you extend yourself on x-c skis. Your conditioning program should be designed to take all of these factors into consideration. Although nearly all x-c skiers find sheer pleasure in traveling across the snow, still there are some who take up the sport simply for its health benefits.

With this in mind, we have organized the book so that you can use it as a basis for learning the sport and then progress to any level you wish. If, for example, you are a runner during the summer, you may find x-c skiing to be a perfect exercise substitute during the winter. But if you want to simply use your skis as a form of transportation in other outdoor activities, you will find information on these subjects as well.

The material on camping can be used separately if all you want to do is drive your car to a camping area or hike on snowshoes.

Since x-c racing is almost a totally different subject, and only a little less technical than automobile racing, it deserves its own book and will not be discussed except in passing.

CHAPTER 2

HISTORY

Cross-country skiing is such a basic form of winter travel and recreation that one wonders why it hasn't consistently been as popular as such activities as ice skating and sledding. But x-c skiing has had a curiously up-and-down record among outdoor enthusiasts. Now that it is well-established throughout Europe and North America, the sport seems destined not only to remain a premier winter activity, but to continue to grow in popularity for some years to come.

Most historians and archaeologists assume snowshoes were the first mode of transportation invented by man for snow travel, simply because they are easier to make than skis. Take a few flexible branches, some rawhide or twigs for the cross pieces, and some kind of thongs to hold them on, and a primitive snowshoe is built. Archaeologists have found various forms of snowshoes all around the Arctic rim, in Tibet, in the Japanese islands, and throughout Europe and North America. For some unknown reason the South American Indians did not develop sophisticated snowshoes nor any form of ski that has been found thus far.

The most highly developed snowshoes were made by the Eskimos and Indians of North America, who used willow, whalebone, sinew, leather, and other materials to create a variety of styles for use in different snow conditions and work situations. Hunting and trapping snowshoes were very long—up to nearly six feet—and

narrow, seldom wider than ten inches. Trail snowshoes were shorter and even narrower, because they were designed to sink deeper in the snow to break trail for dog teams. Thus, it seems that the development of snowshoes was one of man's first technological advances.

However, the development of skis has been fairly recent; the oldest wooden skis found thus far date back only some 5,000 years. The shape and size of cross-country skis have changed very little since then. A petroglyph found on the west coast of Norway shows a man wearing long skis with upturned toes; except for the length of the skis and the exaggerated upturned toes, this could be the silhouette of a modern ski.

The word "ski" came from Northern Europe and originally described a splinter cut from a log. It also became the Scandinavian term for "shoe," which was pronounced "shee."

The first recorded mention of skis is found in the written works of a man named Snoore, whose sagas of the Vikings told of excellent skiers.

The earliest known skis were made

of wood; straps of bark, straw, or leather fastened through vertical holes to hold each foot on the ski. Some models were made of long pieces of hollowed-out wood and looked like canoes with platforms for the feet.

The earliest skiers used one long pole for balance and braking instead of the two poles that came into use sometime in the 18th or 19th century. Those first single poles that skiers used to move and balance themselves sometimes doubled as a hunting lance. It is assumed that the two-pole system originated only when skiers began racing and needed a unique pole especially for that form of recreation.

The first bindings were simply straps of leather or some kind of fabric that held the foot on the ski. An early woodcut of a skier shows him wearing a type of shoe with a toe that is turned up high enough to keep the foot hooked under the ski strap.

The development of ski waxes is also lost in history, but it is assumed that pitch from conifers and various tar substances were used. The Scandinavians compensated for the lack of suitable waxes by developing an unmatched set of skis, one quite long, the other very short. The short ski was called the **andur**, which means "to go;" this was the power ski, the one used for pushing. It was either coated with a resin—tar or pitch—or with a piece of animal skin,—seal or reindeer—to provide traction. The longer ski was polished to a high gloss so the skier could glide along on downhill runs, keeping the power ski either lifted clear of the snow or tucked back on the gliding ski.

the Eskimos and Indians, but they remained crude in comparison to their European and Asian counterparts, perhaps because the North Americans came to depend more on sled dogs and snowshoes.

Except for advances made in materials, ski design has actually changed very little from the days of our ancestors. In fact, skiers apparently still used the single long pole until 1840, when a Lapland skier won a x-c race using two shorter poles instead of the one

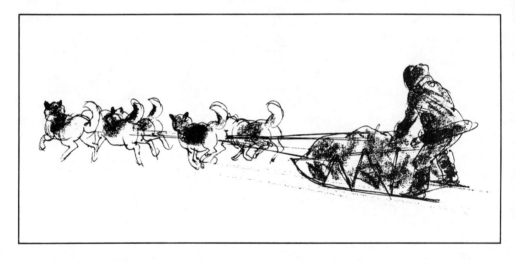

Necessity caused some Arctic residents to become very sophisticated in their types of skis. The Siberians, for example, used more different types of skis than any other people; the mark of a good hunter was that he could judge which kind of ski to use for certain snow conditions. In one area of Siberia noted for its fluffy snow, the Eskimos developed a very wide and short ski that kept them from sinking into the snow yet gave them excellent mobility.

For some reason, ski technology spread all across Europe and Asia but not North America. Skis were used by

crossbow. At about the same time, a writer named Sondre Norheim discovered how to jump and land on a slope rather than flat ground, inventing ski jumping.

By the late 1800s, Scandinavian immigrants had brought many pairs of their long skis to America, and soon ski meets were being held in California's Sierra Nevadas. A ski club named the Alturas Snowshoe Club was formed in 1867, only six years after the first known ski club was formed in Norway.

One of the landmark events in x-c skiing occurred in 1890, when Fridjof Nansen wrote the book, **Crossing**

Greenland on Skis, which told about his trek across the Greenland icecap two years earlier on 12-foot-long wooden skis.

This event inadvertently led to the separation of Nordic (cross-country) skiing and Alpine (downhill) skiing. An Austrian named Mathias Zdarsky read Nansen's book and set to work developing the new sport for his area in the Alps. He developed the "S" turn using the snowplow and stem techniques, and he was the first to use metal, mechanical bindings that could be adjusted to various-sized boots.

Apparently x-c skiing was not really established in America until the middle of the last century, after the first wave of Scandinavian immigrants arrived. Despite this early lack of popular acceptance, a few x-c skiers became legendary figures in the American West, particularly in the Rockies and Sierra Nevada ranges.

One such skier was a minister in Colorado, Father Hyder, who skied to preach and deliver the mail. Another pioneer was A. Bart Henderson, who built a toll road through Yellowstone Canyon in the early 1880s and skied to Bozeman on his "15-foot snow-shoes."

After this slow start, x-c skiing finally gained acceptance in America. The first x-c ski club on record was founded in Minnesota in the late 1880s. California, in keeping with its reputation of being in the forefront of new developments, fads, and crazes, claims the record for the earliest widespread use of x-c skis. The first popular use of the long snowshoes was in about 1850 at the mining camps near LaPorte. Six years later, the legendary Snowshoe Thompson delivered mail from Placerville, California, to Carson City, Nevada, carrying a heavy rucksack of mail on his 94-mile treks. Other areas, particularly Idaho, had legendary x-c skiers as well.

Scandinavian folklore and history are also laden with stories of great feats by skiers. One of Sweden's most popular events is the annual "Wasalopp," an 86-kilometer (53-mile) contest from Salen to Mora. This race commemorates an event that occurred in 1520 when Gustav Eriksson Vasa, a wide-ranging skier, roused the Swedes to rebel against the Danish king. Vasa was crowned King of Sweden in 1523 for these efforts.

Cross-country skiing has had such military applications for several centuries. Scandinavian troops were trained on skis during the winter, just as they were trained on foot during the summer. The soldiers of Northern Europe—Russia, Finland, Norway, and Sweden—were put on skis as part of their standard equipment. For more than five hundred years, from 1300 to 1800, ski troops were a standard military force.

The first military competition held on skis was in Norway in 1767. This event consisted of four exercises: shooting while skiing at full speed downhill; skiing through a deep wooded section; skiing down steep hills without poles; and running x-c while carrying a pack and rifle.

Skis naturally became part of northern peoples' weaponry in times of war. No better illustration exists than the three-month "Winter War" between Russia and Finland during 1939-40.

Just after the Russians had "annexed" Estonia, Latvia, and Lithuania, they expected to invade Finland and Lapland and gain control within two

weeks. Years later, Nikita Khruschev said he had thought that if the Russians would simply raise their voices that "the Finns would put up their hands and surrender." Instead, it took Russia 105 days and one and a half million troops (only 500,000 of whom survived) to defeat the Finns, who were outnumbered 42 to 1 and had no tanks, half-tracks, or heavy artillery.

All the Finns did have was an intimate knowledge of their country, an expertise in traveling on snow, and a hatred of anyone who invaded their country. They equipped themselves with small arms, excellent x-c skis, and bed sheets or any other white cloth that would work as camouflage in the snow. They attacked from the side and the rear during periods of whiteouts and savage blizzards.

The Russians were not prepared for this kind of warfare and found that their heavy equipment was not only useless but dangerous as well, because the Finns could travel anywhere on snow while the armored equipment had to stay on roads.

In the end, of course, the Russians won the war. But one Russian general, sick of the whole debacle, admitted that "we won only enough ground to bury our dead."

Cross-country skiing in North America owes much of its popularity to this and other legendary tales that came out of World War II. Americans saw the Norwegian resistance fighters operate using silent, shadowy skis rather than motor vehicles. Troops in the Alps traveled on downhill skis as well as the Nordic x-c skis. A romanticism developed, and it wasn't long after the war ended that more and more x-c skis began appearing in North America. Some experts in Nordic ski manufacturing even moved to America to help popularize the new sport.

Cross-country didn't grow as rapidly as downhill skiing, just as backpacking hasn't been as popular as organized camping. But with crowded ski slopes, increasing costs of lift tickets, and long lift lines, more and more Americans have taken up cross-country. This is especially true now that x-c skis are becoming more versatile and can perform many of the same functions as downhill skis.

Although x-c skiing is thought of by Americans as a form of recreation, there are many people in the northern regions who treat their skis much as they do their shoes or boots. During the severe winter snowstorms and blizzards that routinely sweep through the Great Lakes states and New England, x-c skis and snowshoes are as common on the streets and parks as bicycles are during the summer months. It is far simpler to step onto a pair of skis than to fuss with the family car by getting it started, putting on chains, and then driving with white knuckles through heavy and dangerous traffic.

Children take to x-c skiing as naturally as they do other forms of self-propelled transportation. And the only requirement for x-c is snow, unlike downhill skiing, which requires a considerable expense and confinement to a specific area.

If these remarks make x-c skiing sound like a new cure-all medicine, it is because now that the sport has taken a firm foothold in North America, many Americans wonder why they didn't "discover" it years ago. This is the mark of an idea—or a sport—whose time has come.

KIDS ON SKIS

If you doubt the truth of the saying that if you can walk, you can ski, watch young children who are learning to ski. They may tumble around a bit and look like mobile snowmen for awhile, but in most cases, children are off and striding across the meadows long before their parents are able to navigate with confidence.

Children are seldom interested in the how-to aspects of anything. Style, technique, nomenclature, jargon—the things in which adults find comfort—tend to make children restless.

Children simply go out and do things the best way they can, so they usually have more fun learning than adults do. Children don't have all the preconceptions and fears that adults have, and their minds are wonderfully devoid of prejudices toward anything that involves activity.

Besides, skiing is just another way of going out to play in the snow.

Of course, the natural exuberance children feel must be tempered somewhat by adult control, lest you spot your child striding and gliding off into the forest wearing only a pair of pajamas. It has happened.

The basic rule in keeping youngsters happy is simple: Keep them warm, dry, and well-fed, all of which are the responsibilities of parents. Children do not learn to be cautious and independent for a number of years, sometimes not until well into their teens.

Most children learn best by experimentation and imitation. It is easier for them to watch someone perform a task and then try it for themselves than to listen to verbal instructions. Thus, follow-the-leader games and instruction techniques will be successful

with them. As they progress on their skis, you can help them organize ball games, tag, relay races, and other games to improve their skills.

The best skis for children are "soft" with very little camber and lots of climbing wax. Better yet, use waxless skis that have lots of kick so the children won't be frustrated by sliding backwards all of the time.

Although parents will always be tempted to overdress their children, they should avoid doing so in cross-country skiing. Cross-country requires more freedom of movement and more exertion than downhill skiing, so you need to dress lighter. However, at the same time you should remember that children can get cold more quickly than adults. Follow the instructions elsewhere in the book to keep children both warm and dry.

Natural fabrics are best for children's outerwear because most synthetics do not permit moisture to "wick" out of the clothing. Wool, goose down, and polypropylene work best for wicking moisture out and away from the skin.

Except during the warm spring weather, children should wear mittens rather than gloves. Mittens are much warmer, permit you to move your fingers around and against each other, and often have interchangeable woolen liners so that you can always keep the inside of the mitten dry.

Children's outerwear should be loose-fitting, water-repellent, and wind-resistant. But don't make your child wear hand-me-downs or grow-intos that are so poorly fitting that the child will trip over them.

Children grow: This is a major problem parents face in all sports. The temptation is to buy inferior equipment or to try to get by with cable ski bindings so that the children can wear work boots or hiking boots rather than authentic ski boots. You will have to make this decision among your own family. Still, it is generally agreed that the traditional three-pin touring boot is best for young skiers, just as it is for you.

Some stores stock equipment designed especially for children, but if this is not available, you may have to buy women's-sized boots for your children.

If you buy used boots, be sure to check them closely. Look for uppers that are separating from soles, enlarged pin holes, and damaged leather. Sole separation and damaged leather can be repaired by a cobbler. But find out first what the repairs will cost because sometimes repairing boots may cost almost as much as buying a new pair; if you add the cost of the used pair and the repair bill, you may spend **more** than on a new pair

If you decide to buy a pair of boots that is slightly too large for the child with the intention of making the boots last at least two seasons, be certain first that you can add sufficient padding—insoles and extra pairs of socks—to make the boots comfortable.

See Chapters 3 and 4 on skis, poles, and other equipment for more information on children's equipment.

PART II
GETTING
READY

CHAPTER 3

CROSS-COUNTRY SKIS

Cross-country skiing has gone the way of all forms of outdoor recreation in that it becomes more and more technical each year. It is nearly impossible now to go shopping for an article of gear without being bewildered by the endless variety of styles, lengths, weights, cambers, waxes, materials, constructions, and brand names.

The sport has become so technical that the challenge is not only how to become conversant in x-c skiing jargon, but how to simplify it for the beginning skier. That is what we hope to do here, while keeping in mind that each person's tastes and needs are different. Thus, it is impossible for any book or outfitter to tell you exactly what kind of equipment you should have.

It's best to start by renting. This is probably the most valuable advice a beginning skier can be given on equipment. For your first year, you may want to rent a package that gives you the option of applying your rental fees toward purchasing equipment.

Do a little research to familiarize yourself with the sport. Read reports on different equipment in skiing magazines and consumer publications. Talk to other x-c skiers and listen to the pros and cons of each type of equipment.

Still, even after receiving advice from experts and friends, the only way you can really determine which equipment is best for you is through your own experience. So, experiment a little. Although waxless skis are becoming more common than waxable ones, you might try both so you'll know without doubt which you prefer. Also experiment with different lengths and widths of skis to find out which is the best for you. Finally, make sure that the equipment you use is for touring, or you'll have more than the normal amount of problems in learning.

It is important to give the rental equipment a good workout so you will become thoroughly familiar with each kind of equpment. Then when you are finally ready to buy, you will be able to do so with confidence.

EQUIPMENT PRIMER

Keeping in mind that each skier has his own preferences and requirements and that industry standards change frequently, the following lists of equipment are suggestions only; they are not carved in stone.

Light Touring
Skis: 46 to 52 mm wide at waist; 0 to 4 mm sidecut; 3 to 4 pounds for 210 cm pair.

Boots: Low-cut like running shoes, often with groove around heel for binding.

Bindings: Aluminum alloy or plastic toepieces about 75 mm wide that attach to front of boot sole, or toe clips about 50 mm wide.

Poles: Most are made of fiberglass now, although Tonkin cane, aluminum, and newer synthetics are being used. Baskets are usually round or asymmetrical and 4 to 5 inches in diameter.

Touring
Skis: 52 to 60 mm wide at waist; 8 to 11 mm sidecut; weighs from 5 to 7 pounds for 210 cm pair. Some have steel or aluminum edges for greater downhill control.

Boots: Above ankle, like hiking boots.

Bindings: 71 to 79 mm wide toepieces of aluminum or hard plastic. Some with heel straps or cables.

Poles: Same as light-touring but with slightly larger baskets.

Ski Mountaineering
Skis: The largest and heaviest made with a waist width of 61 mm or wider; 9 to 12 mm sidecut. Usually weigh more than 6 pounds for 210 cm pair. Steel or aluminum edges.

Boots: Similar in construction to summer mountaineering boots with two-layer construction for greater insulation.

Bindings: Either wider versions of the touring bindings or with Alpine (downhill) type of quick release.

Poles: Same as touring.

SKIS

The typical pair of x-c skis is longer, narrower, and lighter than downhill skis. The basic shapes are only slightly different, except that x-c skis are turned up a bit at the rear as well as the front.

In many ways, x-c skis are more of a precision instrument than downhill skis because they are manufactured not only for your specific height and weight, but also for the specific kind of skiing you intend to do. There is enough variation among these categories so that you can use the same skis for touring and recreational racing, but not so much latitude that you should use touring skis for mountaineering.

PACKS

Lightweight day touring

Overnight

Ski mountaineering

WEIGHTS AND MEASURES

If you don't know a centimeter from a centipede, you have lots of company in your confusion over ski lengths and weights. For some reason the ski industry has largely ignored the metric system of weights and continued to use the English system of ounces and pounds.

Anyway, here's a conversion chart to get you started:

If You Know:	And You Want:	Multiply By:
Inches	Centimeters	2.54
Feet	Centimeters	30.48
Yards	Meters	0.91
Miles	Kilometers	1.61
Quarts	Liters	0.95
Gallons	Liters	3.76
Ounces	Grams	28.35
Pounds	Kilograms	0.45

(If you know Centimeters And you want inches Multiply by .3937)

Thus, when you see skis listed as 210 cm, they are 82.6 inches long or 6.8 feet.

CAMBER AND FLEX

If you place a x-c ski on a table or counter, you will note that it doesn't lie flat. The center section, where you will stand, is thicker and curves up slightly. This is called the "camber," and it is necessary in order to distribute your weight evenly over the length of the ski.

The ski tip should bend up and down with relative ease; this is called the "flex." You need enough flex to permit the tip to flow over varied terrain, but not so much that you lose stability.

These two features affect traction, so they are among the most important considerations when buying a pair of skis. Be sure to get assistance from a store clerk who knows skis well.

Most skis are manufactured with camber and flex set according to length, based on the average weight of the person who needs that specific length. But if you're either lighter or heavier than the average person of your height, you will have to make adjustments. Sometimes you can find skis with a variety of camber and flex equations, like you can buy boots in various widths within the same size. But it isn't always easy to find these variations, so you may have to buy skis either longer or shorter than those recommended for your height.

There's no guaranteed method of finding your proper camber and flex other than going out on the snow for several sessions. But the industry has devised a method that is sufficient for most purposes: the paper test.

To perform this test, take a sheet of paper about four or five inches wide and place it under the middle of one ski on a hard, uncarpeted floor. Next, stand on the ski. The paper should be held to the floor. If the paper can be moved easily, the skis are too stiff; but if the paper can't be moved at all, the skis are too limber.

Another test that some racing skiers use for the camber is to place a pair of skis together, bottom to bottom, and press. If you can flatten them together with both hands, they are approximately right for you. Using one hand, you should almost be able to bring them together. If you can completely bring them together with only one hand, they're too soft; if you can't do it at all, even using two hands, they're too stiff. Admittedly, this is probably the least scientific of the methods, but some skiers swear by it.

MATERIALS

Today, virtually all skis are made of synthetic fiber plastics. However, a small percentage are still made of laminated wood for the minority of skiers who not only believe that wood is superior, but who prefer the look and feel of natural materials to that of the machine-tooled plastics.

Plastics have taken over for a variety of reasons. Primarily, plastic is more durable, easier to work with, and both lighter and stronger. It is also more dependable than wood, which tends to be a bit unpredictable. But, as with other types of equipment, personal taste becomes the final element in your decision on which material to buy, regardless of an unemotional listing of the pros and cons or an impassioned lecture by an expert.

Wood Considerations

Wooden skis are usually composed of five to eight kinds of wood, laminated with the grains reversed to help prevent warping. The major woods used are hickory, birch, beech, ash, poplar, spruce, balsa, and obeche. These layers are held together with water-resistant epoxies, resins, and other glue compounds. An excellent pair of wooden skis may contain more than 30 layers of different woods. Often these layers are arranged so that the strongest woods are on the top and bottom, providing load carrying ability, and the lighter, more flexible woods are used in the middle layers.

The major problem with wooden

SKI REPAIR KIT

Clothing and tent repairs: A large sewing needle or sewing awl with nylon thread or dental floss will take care of most rips and tears.

Ski poles: Duct tape and perhaps a thin strip of sheet metal to wrap around the poles before taping.

Replacing screws: Epoxy works well, provided you have a heat source so the resin will set properly. Also be sure to carry a screwdriver with the proper head to fit the screws on your skis.

Vice grips: These can be used as pot-holders, clamps for repairs, and wire cutters.

Extra equipment: Bring along spare ski tips, pack clevis pins, pole baskets, and binding parts, such as bails.

skis is the base, since this is where most of the wear occurs. If the base covering is worn away, moisture enters the wood and creates havoc through freezing, thawing, and swelling. Some skis have a base of resin-impregnated wood to prevent this.

Another problem is the technology involved in building first-rate skis from a material which, due to grain and similar characteristics, seems to have a mind of its own. Wood isn't as easily adapted as synthetic materials, so the manufacturing process is always more complex.

Synthetic Materials

As noted above, synthetic skis have virtually captured the market. This is mainly because mass production is much simpler, so the price remains lower.

Such a wide variety of plastic is used that you would have to be a chemist or engineer to understand the structural advantages and disadvantages of each type of synthetic. What's more, the list of plastics and construction techniques continues to grow with

---

SAFETY CHECKLIST

- Be in good physical condition.
- Begin skiing short distances and gradually extend your trips.
- Stay within your capabilities.
- Always travel with at least one other person.
- On overnight trips. leave a message with someone that tells them where you're going and when you expect to return. Then be certain to notify them when you do return.
- Always carry basic emergency items with you, even on short day trips.
- Listen to weather forecasts and always expect the worst.
- In case you get caught in bad weather—snowstorm, whiteout, or hard wind—seek shelter rather than try to force your way through.
- If you get lost, stop and force yourself to remain calm. Decide if it is safer to continue or to hole up and wait for help.

---

each season. Whereas wood technology appears to have reached the state of the art, synthetic technology appears to have much more potential. Consumers are eagerly accepting all sorts of new ski designs. Some skis are constructed of several types of plastic, while others include air tubes inside them to both lighten the skis and give a bit more cushion in the flex. New edges are being tried to help improve telemarking so that the boundary between cross-country and downhill skiing is blurred even more. Thus, a comment that a certain process is "the latest and greatest improvement" is probably out of date before the ink is dry.

Still, the two basic kinds of synthetic construction remain sandwich and box. "Sandwich" construction means the top and base are of a harder, denser plastic, because this is where the load is carried and the most wear occurs. A lighter material, often a dense foam, is injected between these outer layers.

"Box" construction creates a stronger ski side than the sandwich technique, so that the sides also bear the load. The box style has much more strength but is also considerably stiffer than the sandwich.

This is only a very basic comparison, because manufacturers have developed numerous variations within these two types and in some cases have blended them so that it is almost impossible to tell the difference. On the one hand, sandwich construction is slightly easier to control during manufacturing, because it is essentially a lamination process and the quality control is easier. But on the other hand, since it is a lamination process, the danger of delamination always exists.

SKI LENGTH

A general rule in determining ski length is to stand flat and hold one arm straight above your body. The correct length of ski should touch your wrist.

The accompanying illustration and chart shows the approximate lengths of skis and poles recommended by the industry. There are many exceptions to these rules, especially regarding individual preferences and the fitting of growing children. It is advisable to use these rules only as approximations while testing several pairs of skis before buying, since body weight also plays a role in selection. Most retailers have guidelines for both height and weight, so you can compute your own length requirements.

TO WAX
OR NOT TO WAX

The subject of wax is one aspect of x-c skiing that will invariably confuse the novice. Some beginners, after listening to lengthy lectures on the subject, have been known to throw up their hands in defeat and swear off x-c skiing for life. So we will try to keep the discussion simple and then move along to less technical matters.

Cross-country skis are designed to let you go uphill, downhill, and across land with little more effort than used when hiking the same terrain in the summer. You will huff and puff a bit going uphill, but going downhill and across the flats will be a breeze.

Obviously what slides forward will also slide backward, and skis—built to slide better than anything else—would

be impossible if not for special waxes and bottom designs. Neither waxable nor waxless skis are perfect, but both are close.

WHEN SPRING COMES

Here are some simple rules for packing away your ski equipment after the snow melts:

- Repair all base, sidewall, and topsheet gouges and delaminations.
- Remove all old wax from the base, and then iron in a new layer of base wax. With waxless skis, apply base wax to tip and tail areas.

Storing your equipment:

- Some skiers prefer a cool, damp storage spot, which is a throwback to the days of wooden skis; other skiers prefer a warm area, because they think the heat helps the wax penetrate the base.
- Store skis flat; do not place anything on top of them to affect the camber or cause warping.
- Check your poles and make repairs if necessary before putting them away. Tape poles together so they won't get lost.
- Apply a waterproofing solution to ski boots once they are dry; then stuff the boots with newspapers to help them maintain their shape.

GUIDE TO APPROXIMATE X-C SKI AND POLE LENGTHS

	Height (feet)	Ski length (cm)	Pole length (cm)
Children	3'5"	120	Poles not
and	3'7"	130	recom-
Junior	3'10"	140	mended
	4'0"	150	90
	4'2"	160	95
	4'5"	170	100
	4'7"	180	105
	4'9"	185	110
	4'10"	190	115
	5'1"	195	120
	5'4"	195	125
	5'6"	200	
Women	4'9"	185	110
	4'11"	185	115
	5'1"	190	120
	5'3"	190	125
	5'5"	195	130
	5'7"	200	135
	5'9"	205	140
	5'10"	210	140
Men	5'1"	195	120
	5'3"	200	125
	5'5"	205	130
	5'7"	210	135
	5'9"	210	140
	5'11"	210	145
	6'1"	215	150
	6'3"	220	155

If it were simply a matter of using skis to climb a hill and then slide back down again, you would have no problem. You could simply attach a pair of crampons or knotted ropes to the ski bottoms, and you would get up almost any hill; you could then take them off and slide back down again.

But x-c skiing is not quite that simple. You want skis that will slide forward with no effort but will not slide backward when you try to move along on level or uphill terrain.

Thanks to the variety of waxes and designs of waxable skis, you can keep moving along, almost as though you were trudging along in your hiking boots. With each step you make a slight stamping motion and the ski bottoms grip.

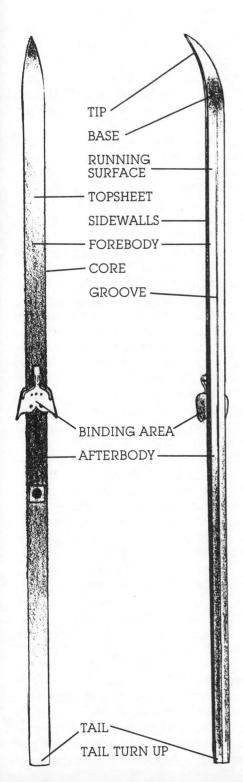

TIP

BASE

RUNNING
SURFACE

TOPSHEET

SIDEWALLS

FOREBODY

CORE

GROOVE

BINDING AREA

AFTERBODY

TAIL

TAIL TURN UP

SKI PARTS

Base: the material on the bottom of skis, which runs the full length, as opposed to;

Running surface (or simply bottom): The part of the base in contact with the snow.

Top: Self-explanatory.

Topsheet: The material on top of the ski.

Sidewalls: The material on the sides between the top and bottom.

Forebody: The forward half of the ski.

Afterbody: The rear half of the ski.

Core: The material between the top, bottom, and sidewalls.

Tip: The forward end of the ski.

Tail: The rear end of the ski.

Shovel: The turned-up-section at the tip of the ski.

Tail Turn-up: The rear turned-up section of the ski.

Groove: The bottom indentation that runs the length of the ski.

Binding area: The indented section on top of the ski for mounting bindings.

Body: The entire ski, minus the turned-up front and rear ends.

Waxless skis are a bit easier to understand. The bottoms of the skis are covered with one of three or four types of material or machine-produced patterns that permit the skis to slide in one direction (forward) but catch on the snow when pushed in the opposite direction. Mohair is one material used; it is attached to the skis with the hair lying flat, pointed toward the tail of the ski. When moving forward, the hair lies flat; when moving backward, the hair catches in the snow and stands on end to act as a brake.

Another base is called the "fish-scale," which uses raised or feathered patterns that are angled slightly backward; tiny ridges at the end of each "scale" work to prevent backward motion without hindering foward motion.

There are also some models of waxless skis to which you apply wax only for certain snow conditions, which sort of imitates the performance of a waxable ski. But most varieties of waxless skis use some bottom design, as described above.

Waxless skis are favored by many x-c skiers who enjoy their sport only in a recreational sense. They like going out in the snow and moving about the countryside, but they don't enjoy constantly fiddling and fussing with their equipment. These skiers don't worry about performance, perfection, and other such matters.

Other skiers find that waxable skis provide superb overall performance, provided you know how and when to wax them. Once you learn the whole waxing procedure, it becomes a major part of the excitement of x-c skiing. Waxing gives you much more control over your equipment, because you can constantly adjust your skis' performance by choosing the proper wax for the given conditions.

Wax and snow have a curious relationship. Waxed skis allow the surface snow to penetrate the wax just far enough to provide a grip, yet permit the skis to glide when they are moving along. Thus, you must understand your snow and your wax to know which combination works best. If you apply wax that is too hard for the snow conditions, you won't get a gripping effect, because the snow won't be able to penetrate the wax. But if you apply wax that is too soft for the snow con-

WAXLESS DOMINATES

Waxless skis have virtually taken over in the popular marketplace, and more professional ski teams use them as well, because they have improved so much over the past few years. The machine-patterned bases have been interestingly modified in search of the perfect design that will give a maximum of both kick and glide.

Some newer waxless designs permit you to adjust the camber of the skis according to the type of snow and terrain you are on, which gives your skis a deeper bite into the snow for kick and climbing.

Although some experts insist that waxable skis are obsolete, they really haven't been consigned to history quite yet. There will always be those who prefer and enjoy waxing, but their numbers are declining.

ditions, the wax will be so sticky that your skis won't glide in any direction.

Manufacturers of ski waxes have gradually developed a series of waxes for each general snow condition and temperature range. The hard waxes, which are for new snow, come in stick form; the more fluid, sticky waxes, or klisters, are for old snow and come in tube form.

The standard waxing system uses these materials:

Preparation waxes, as the name implies, provide the undercoating over which other specific-use waxes are built. For wooden skis, an impregnation type of wax is used to both protect the skis and to help the next coat adhere. On plastic skis, a paraffin wax is used in the preparation phase to give a protective coating to the base and to improve glide.

Base waxes are the second layer of wax; they further protect the ski base and serve as a binding agent for the specialized wax. Hard-base wax can be used for all types of final waxes, and a base klister is used when klister will be the final layer.

Final waxes are those that make contact with the snow. The hard waxes are used for dry snow; klister waxes are used for moist, new snow and at freezing temperatures. Plain klister wax works on wet or coarse snow and on icy tracks; and glide wax helps increase the glide on plastic-based skis.

Cleaners, obviously, are solvents used to remove the old wax.

Keep in mind that endless research has been done on the subject of waxes; there is a lot to learn. So, if you're still new to the sport and trying to decide if this is how you want to spend your winters, you can make that first season—or those yet to come—rel-atively simple by using a two-wax system. This isn't as scientific as experimenting with the whole gamut of wax colors and types, but your skis will get you there and back just the same, without cluttering your mind with a seminar on waxes.

This basic system uses one wax for temperatures above freezing and another for temperatures below freezing. It is as simple as that—almost. There is always a catch, and this is a rather mild one: You must apply the wax in very thin layers. The system is flexible enough so that you can apply the colder wax at the start of the day and then add a layer of the warmer wax as the day progresses. Or you can just stick with one wax all day.

As your skill improves and your enthusiasm for the sport grows, you can work your way into the more complex wax system. And when you do, you will at first be struck by the bewildering selection of beautifully packaged and colored cans and tubes of waxes.

This color coding has a purpose other than decoration. The colder colors—green and blue—are for use on colder days; warmer colors—purple, yellow, red, and so forth—are for warmer days.

This sounds simple, too, but there are a host of subtle differences to contend with. Snow is hardly ever the same from day to day, week to week; hence, the Eskimos' vast vocabulary of words to describe different kinds of snow. The day may be warm, but the snow may be old and refrozen, with a sheen of melt on top of the crust. Or the southern slopes may be soft while the northern slopes are still rather crusty.

To be effective in these different types of snow, each kind of wax must be applied properly. Some must be

The master x-c skier, John Caldwell, offers these words of advice on waxing:

- Learn how to use one brand of wax thoroughly before branching out and trying another line.
- Always use hard wax for snow that is in its original state; use klisters for snow that has melted and refrozen.
- Begin waxing with a warm, dry ski in a warm room.
- Choose a wax by using the outside air temperature as a guide; than follow the temperature range instructions printed on the wax container's label.
- Don't be afraid to experiment.
- Keep an account of your waxing results in your head or, even better, in a little diary-notebook tucked in your pocket.

WAX INGREDIENTS

What is a ski wax made of? Small amounts of several things: petroleum wax is used for water repellency; synthetic rubber is used for adhesion; oil and Vaseline are used to soften hard waxes; and synthetic resin is used to soften sticky klister waxes. The various waxes use different percentages of these basic ingredients to achieve the desired quality.

applied in thin layers, while others will need to be thick. If the snow conditions are such that you could use one of several waxes, you can melt them together and then apply them as one. Complete familiarity with waxes and experience with the various kinds of snow will turn most x-c skiers into instinctive waxers. And the varieties for the experts are endless.

How to Apply Wax

Here again, we must keep this discussion rather general to avoid writing a textbook that will soon be rendered useless by new developments in ski waxes and techniques. But it isn't as complicated as it sounds.

Hard waxes are the easiest to apply. Simply treat a wax stick like a crayon, using the edge of the wax for a smoother layer. Then grasp your cork pad and rub the wax with short, vigorous strokes to even it and ensure a good hold on the skis.

Klister is a bit more tricky to use because it is almost a form of glue and will cling to anything it touches. The tube should be warmed slightly. You can probably hold it in your hand awhile to get it soft enough, but if you are applying it out on the trail in cold weather, you'll need a torch to warm it. After it has softened, apply the wax by pressing the nozzle of the tube against the ski and squeezing a ribbon down each side of the groove. A spreader comes with the wax, and should be used to apply it evenly. You may also need a rag to clean up the spills and runs.

Klister wax, as opposed to plain klister, is a hard wax that comes in a can yet is still very sticky. It will refuse to cooperate and you must be prepared for a mess—keep rags handy.

Spread the wax out with a torch, rags, or a piece of cork that you don't mind throwing away.

Some waxes do not have to be applied to any area of the ski other than the kicker zone, or the cambered section beneath your feet. Others must be applied the full length of the ski. Whatever the case, when heat is needed few things work better than a plain old steam iron. Most skiers become quite adept at this basic technique.

As it stands now—and perhaps will for some time—both waxable and waxless skis have their definite places in the sport. There will always be those who enjoy the preparation involved with waxable skis almost as much as

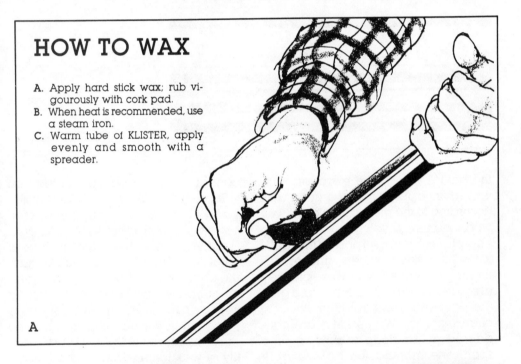

HOW TO WAX

A. Apply hard stick wax; rub vigourously with cork pad.
B. When heat is recommended, use a steam iron.
C. Warm tube of KLISTER, apply evenly and smooth with a spreader.

A

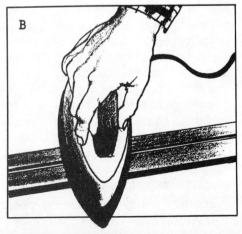

B

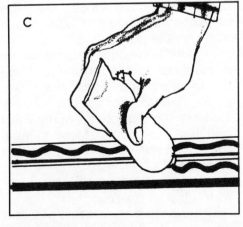

C

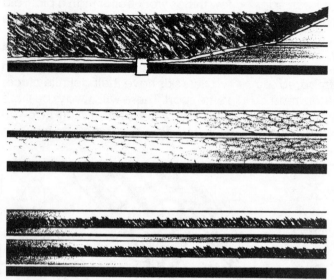

WAXLESS SKI BOTTOMS VARY IN CONFIGURATION

top—Mohair. middle—Fish-scale pattern. bottom—Mohair inserts.

the actual skiing. The extra effort involved in applying the proper wax according to the snow conditions is well worth the time involved for those who enjoy it. So, it is not surprising that dedicated x-c skiers, racers, and manufacturers swear by waxable skis. They are faster on downhill slopes and give the skier more control over the skis' characteristics. Waxless skis are considered a handicap to enjoying the sport; one manufacturer of waxable skis said that using waxless skis is the equivalent of playing 18 holes of golf with only the putter.

But for beginners, children, occasional skiers, and those who just want to step onto a pair of skis to run down to the mailbox, waxless skis are fine. They serve a purpose for many skiers and make skiing no more complicated than putting on a pair of boots or overshoes.

Which is Best for You?

After putting aside all the pros and cons of the two basic types of skis, you will probably know which kind of skis you will want, just through your own experience with other sports.

If you enjoy things that require a lot of "fine tuning" and if you like having complete control over your equipment, you will probably enjoy waxing your own skis. It will give you pleasure to go out in the morning and test the snow to determine the kind and quantity of wax to use. Then, when you return in the evening, part of your fun will be to dress down the skis again in preparation for the next day's outing.

But if you simply want a pair of skis that you can step onto and take off, you're a candidate for the waxless. The overall performance of skis and the technical aspects of the activity mean less to you than getting out and skiing.

This may be something of an oversimplification, because people don't always exactly fit into either category. But for the beginning skier, it is a good way to approach decision making.

CHAPTER 4

BOOTS, BINDINGS, AND POLES

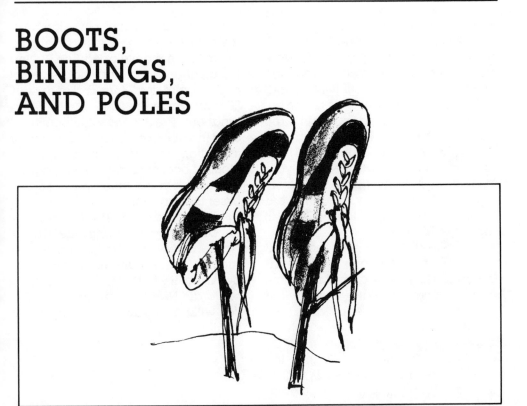

The first cross-country skis were built to attach to ordinary cold-weather boots, using bindings no more scientific than leather straps with buckles. The first metal bindings were developed in the 1930s and were made like roller skates, having adjustable clamps for the toes of the boots and straps around the heels to hold the toes snugly in the clamps. Similar bindings are still in use today, especially the spring bindings that push the toe forward into the clamp.

Toe bindings have gradually become the accepted method of attaching boots to skis. Both boots and bindings are designed to be a working unit; one is made for the other.

Now virtually all x-c boots have an extension from the front of the sole called the "snout." The binding is attached to the snout in a variety of methods. Some snouts have vertical holes into which pins or spikes from the bindings fit. This makes it virtually impossible to lose your skis, especially with the clamp holding the toe in place against the ski.

Most new boots and bindings do not bother with the heel of the boot, except to provide guides on the skis where the heel will fit. The heel should be free for up-and-down motion while striding along, but the side motion should be virtually nil.

To prevent this lateral motion, some boots and bindings have a plate on the heel. These plates can be nothing more than serrated metal or hard plastic to give the boot heel a grip.

Others are wedges of metal or plastic that fit into a slot in the boot heel. Either type permits you to exert pressure against the ski for turns, climbing, and other maneuvers, without twisting your ankle or slipping your boot off the ski.

Boots and bindings come in three major systems: the Nordic Norm, the Racing Norm, and Norm 38. These uniform systems guarantee that your boots and bindings will be completely compatible and that you can have a wide choice of boots that will still fit the same bindings.

The Nordic Norm is the most common type for recreational skiing. It has a single-sized snout and binding but three choices of width. These width variations involve the distance between the pins and pin recesses on the boots and bindings. Common widths are 71 mm, 75 mm, and 79 mm; the most common is the 75 mm. Actually, these measurements make little or no difference to most skiers and have practically no bearing on the kind they buy. However, remember that each binding and boot must be the same measurement.

The Nordic Norm was the first standard boot-and-binding system adopted by manufacturers to simplify the selection process for consumers. It appeared in the 1920s and was the accepted standard for more than forty years. Then, in the 1960s, racing became very popular, and skis and boots became both narrower and lighter, necessitating additional standards. Thus, the Racing Norm and a similar system called Norm 38 were developed.

The Racing Norm became more popular during the 1970s, as more people became expert at the sport. The 75 mm-wide boots and skis seemed awkward and clumsy, so the narrower systems of the Racing Norm and Norm 38 were developed. The Racing Norm had two major thicknesses of boots, 12 mm and 7 mm, and one width, 50 mm; hence, the 50/12 and 50/7 designations. The thinner-soled boots created the disadvantage of having poor insulation against the cold, but new types of boot construction with sophisticated foam insulation have helped offset that problem.

To summarize, you will most likely be concerned only with the Nordic Norm, unless you are going into ski racing. So the main thing to remember is that if you buy skis with bindings of Nordic Norm 75 mm, for example, you will have to buy boots of the same family.

TYPES OF BINDINGS

Aside from the three systems discussed, there are still many other kinds of bindings. Many x-c skiers remain loyal to their old bindings, which adjust for a variety of boot widths and sizes.

Toe bindings are similar to the roller skate bindings, as they clamp just to the front of your boots.

Cable bindings use a similar toe clamp, except that it does not clasp the boot sole so tightly. Instead, it is held in place by a cable that is passed around the heel of the boot. Some of these bindings are simply springs with cables attached, and others have ratchet-loaded clamps for tension. These are popular with skiers who head for the mountains and other tough terrain, because they are the

BOOTS & BINDINGS

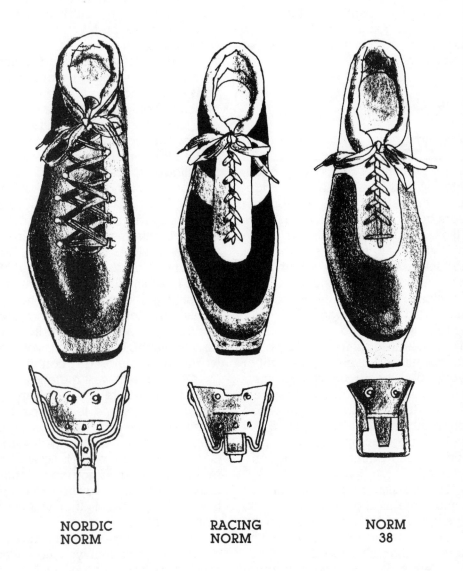

NORDIC
NORM

RACING
NORM

NORM
38

firmest bindings. By the same token, they are often the most difficult to get out of after a fall.

Which type is best for you? There's no simple answer to that question, and it is one only you can answer for yourself. Again, if possible, try several types before buying; rent them for weekends, exchange skis with companions, and talk to your x-c ski shop owner for recommendations.

BOOTS

So many types of boots are available now that nobody can adequately cover the subject. Just a few years ago, boot manufacturers were quite rigid in their models and made only what they thought was best for most skiers. Factors such as individual taste, insulation from the cold, and variations in thickness were not addressed as they are today.

Now there are no apparent limits within these systems. You can buy boots that are stiff or flexible, lightweight or heavy, padded or unpadded, insulated for Arctic climates or for barely freezing temperatures. But the most important thing to remember is to buy boots that are compatible with your bindings and at the same time comfortable.

The best fitting boots should be as comfortable as a good pair of walking shoes. They should be snug around the heel to avoid slipping, yet not so snug that they become uncomfortable. There should be adequate room in the toe so that circulation is not impeded, but not so much room that your feet slide around in them. Keep

in mind how many pairs of socks you will wear in the boots, and have your normal sock complement with you when you try the boots on. Walk around the store to check the fit, flex them, and kneel in them. You might be able to enjoy yourself with skis that aren't exactly right for you, but if your boots make your feet hurt, you won't enjoy anything on an outing.

Most boots are designed to keep your feet warm under normal conditions, which includes temperatures at or slightly below zero Fahrenheit. If you are going on tougher expeditions, such as mountaineering trips or in weather that is substantially colder, you should investigate special boots and bindings for Arctic conditions. Some of these "overboots" are actually insulated gaiters. Sometimes when the conditions are extreme, such as in parts of the United States and northern Canada and Alaska, you will need the Arctic-rated shoe paks, which are often adapted for snowmobile use. They are made much larger than normal boots and have inserts made of felt or synthetic materials that will keep your toes warm under almost any conditions.

One of the newest materials used in x-c boots is Gore-Tex. It began as a fabric for coats and tents because it allows moisture to be wicked outward from the body, yet it is waterproof. Gore-Tex has made boots lighter and more flexible. And since they breathe, drawing moisture away from the body, they keep your feet drier when you work up a sweat.

Another factor to consider is to have a pair of boots that you can wear around the camp or lodge while you give your feet a rest and also dry out your other boots. Many brands of modified mukluks are available that

BOOTS

Heavyduty backcountry touring boots—good for off-track wilderness.

Beginner's boots—padded snow cuff.

For the serious x-c skier—padded snow cuff—fleece lined—designed for downhill and telemark control.

Goose down booties for after-ski and tent wear.

will keep your feet and ankles warm while walking on snow. These mukluks are usually calf-length and made of a soft leather or synthetic material from the foot up, with a harder sole for long wear and traction on the snow.

Slipper socks, usually made of wool with a leather sole, are good for relaxing in a lodge, cabin, or tent. Most have soft leather soles and are like wearing a pair of soft moccasins with heavy wool socks. You can keep these on in the sleeping bag, unless you have along a pair of goose-down booties, to keep your feet warm at night.

SKI TIP

Clean socks are essential for comfort. When you perspire, your body releases salt; this collects in your socks and acts as a sponge for moisture. Some skiers are convinced that fabric softeners have the same effect as salt and will not use them when washing their socks.

POLES

Poles are one of the easiest purchases you will make, because there are very few kinds. However, you should consider the following factors when buying your ski poles.

Materials

Poles are made of three basic materials: synthetic fiber, aluminum, and Tonkin cane. As with skis, synthetics have become quite popular, because

they are less likely to bend than aluminum and less likely to break and splinter than Tonkin cane.

Parts of the Pole

Grips are made of a variety of materials, including cork, leather, and a selection of synthetics ranging from velour to simulated leather. Cork, leather, and simulated leather are the most preferred because they absorb hand perspiration rather than get slippery and are warmer to the touch.

Straps are made of several materials, both natural and synthetic. It is helpful to have adjustable straps so you can lower or raise them according to changing snow conditions. Some poles are designed to be used as left and right, so look at the straps to make sure you get a matched set.

Baskets are the circular piece which is attached near the tip of the pole. Most have a high vinyl content so they won't harden or crack in the cold. The type and size of basket you get will depend upon the kind of snow you want to ski on. To be safe, buy a pair of poles with four-inch baskets, which are best for skiing on snow-packed trails. Then get a set of baskets that are an inch or more larger and can be clipped onto the existing size basket; these larger baskets work well for skiing in looser, unpacked snow. The type of baskets should be a major consideration in choosing poles, so examine them carefully.

Ferrules are a strengthening addition to the lower end of the pole and provide a base for the tip.

Tips are usually made of a steel alloy for durability. They are sometimes straight or curved slightly for ease in removing them from the snow and providing additional push. They are

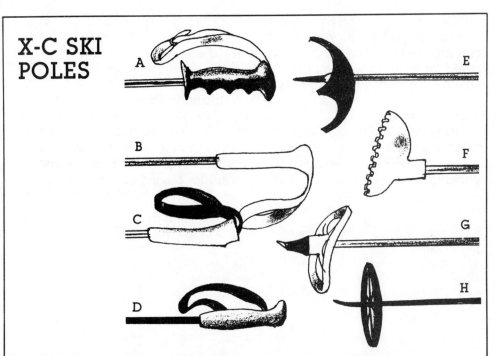

X-C SKI POLES

A   B   C   D   E   F   G   H

(A) Finger-form molded grip. **(B)** One-piece molded grip. **(C)** Contoured molded grip. **(D)** Variation on grip shaped to fit hand. **(E-H)** Variety of baskets, both rigid and flexible, are available to meet a skier's perceived need for a change as terrains vary. **Note**—Some poles are designed for a secondary function. Remove handles and baskets, screw two poles together and you have an avalanche probe.

often screwed into the ferrule and can be sharpened with a file.

Length

The easiest way to determine the proper length for a ski pole is to stand with your feet flat on the floor and raise one arm straight out from your body. The pole that fits comfortably under that arm will be about the right length for you.

Don't try to use your downhill ski

SKI TIP

The best way to grip your pole is to reach up through the strap, as though you are going to let the pole dangle from your wrist. Then drop your hand on top of the strap, with your thumb on one side and your fingers on the other, and grip the pole. This grip gives you the ability to push down and back on the strap and pole.

When you grip the pole by dropping your hand down through the strap, you have nothing to push against and your hand will slip off the pole easily.

poles for x-c skiing; each type is used differently, because your arm movements are different. Longer poles are needed for x-c, because you depend on them for part of your propulsion.

Children's Poles

Nearly all children's poles have plastic tips for safety. They are usually made of less expensive materials but are available in all the major types: Tonkin cane, aluminum, and plastic. When deciding the correct pole length for a child, choose one that is a bit short.

Avalanche Safety Tip

Many poles now can be screwed together to serve as avalanche probes. If you plan to ski in avalanche-prone areas, such as the West, you should consider buying this type of pole.

CHAPTER 5

CLOTHING

There's no escaping the pressures of fashion, even miles away from the nearest trailhead, because all of us are subject to the plumage syndrome in one form or another. Since we are the only species without natural wool or feathers, we spend a great deal of time worrying about what kind of protective covering to wear.

Cross-country skiers used to tend to dress alike, wearing something on the order of a winter uniform that consisted of baggy knickers, high wool socks with gaiters, vividly patterned Scandinavian sweaters, and long, loose parkas.

Choosing clothing is almost as bewildering to the novice as is the selection of skis and boots. In addition to the old standbys of densely woven woolens, we have blends of wool and synthetic fibers, synthetic piles, newer lightweight wind- and waterproof fabrics, and so forth. And, as if this weren't enough to worry about, we still feel compelled to dress according to the latest fashions, because—like it or not—we are still initially judged by our appearance.

Of course there remain a few renegades on the trails who do not care a bit for fashion. They wear the same clothing, winter after winter, and feel as loyal to it as they do the tattered sweater or mangled moccasins that everyone else in the family wants to burn.

So, we won't discuss fashions and fads, because such information could easily be out of date before this book

THE LAYERING SYSTEM

appears. (You can select your own color schemes and labels.) Instead, we will concentrate on that old standby of outdoor dressing, the layering system.

The layering system is the only method of dressing for cold weather that really works. As an example, suppose you are wearing a wool shirt underneath a parka that is rated to well below zero. It is below freezing when you put on your skis and take off for the timber. But by noon the sun is hot and you have to shed the parka. After you ski a few minutes, though, you find that the wool shirt isn't quite warm enough. So there you are with a too-

cold and too-hot combination, neither of which is sufficient. If you wear the parka, you work up a sweat that chills you, but if you take off the parka, you're faced with the threat of hypothermia.

Take a look, though, at your companion. He is wearing a waffle-weave set of underwear, a lightweight wool shirt, a pullover sweater, and a lightweight parka. As the day warms up, he takes off the parka, removes the sweater, and then puts the parka back on. Or he can take the parka off and leave the sweater on. He has one more layer of clothing than you do, so he can fine-tune his comfort range without being either too hot or too cold.

Although Eskimos are known for their magnificent hand-sewn fur par-

kas, this type of heavyweight clothing by itself is really not the best for the Arctic conditions. Instead, the best is layers of clothing, as described above. Eskimos also wear long, pullover parkas called "anoraks," which come to the knee and are the last article of clothing put on. They are frequently rather thin but are made of closely woven fabrics so they serve as windbreakers more than anything else. Some parkas used in Canada and Alaska have zip-out linings of goose down or wool so that they can be adapted to the various seasons and temperature changes.

The secret to this layering system

is that "dead" air is trapped between the layers, providing insulation from outside temperatures. One layer traps some air, two layers traps more air, and so on. This is the same principle that makes goose down the best insulator known; the down itself doesn't keep you warm, but the air trapped by the down does.

It is impossible to tell each individual how to dress because each person's metabolic rate is different; some of us are more susceptible to cold or heat than others. But here is a basic layering system that will suffice for most winter trips and may even be too much for some conditions. It is only an example, so you can add or subtract layers according to your own needs.

First Layer: you should wear thermal net (waffle-weave) long johns against your skin. These long johns wick sweat away from your body so that it won't evaporate against your skin and cool you. The net construction creates dead-air spaces close to the skin to hold air warmed by your body.

Make sure to consider the type of material used. Cotton is not a good cold-weather clothing material because it tends to keep the moisture against your skin; it also traps salt, which retains moisture, too. Wool is the best material for retaining heat, even when wet, but it can cause discomfort when against the skin. Synthetics, such as polypropylene, are the most popular.

In addition to these long johns, you should also wear your normal underwear. And on your feet your first layer should be a silk or light polyester sock that wicks the moisture away from your feet into the outer layer of socks.

Second Layer: this layer begins with a second pair of socks, such as a heavy wool pair. Next, a wool or wool-blend turtleneck sweater may be added over your long johns. Or just wear a wool shirt. Finally, you need a pair of wool pants.

Wool is continually emphasized because of its ability to provide warmth while wet. However, several modern synthetics are now capable of the same effect, too.

Outer Layer: from the feet up, this final layer contains boots, gaiters, light and closely woven windpants that fit loosely and are tucked in at the waist and ankles, a sweater over your shirt, a wind parka, head gear, and hand coverings.

SKI TIP

Always put on dry, clean socks once you have arrived at your skiing destination. Wear causes socks to compress and lose their insulation value, and your feet have probably been blasted by the car's heater, causing them to sweat. Don't start out your ski trip wearing these dirty, damp socks.

Many, if not most, skiers wear insulated gloves, often with a sheer liner for additional warmth and moisture wicking. However, mittens are still the best choice for extremely cold weather. Good mittens usually consist of a leather shell with thick woolen inserts that can be be changed as they get wet from perspiration or melted snow.

So much of your body temperature escapes from your neck and scalp, where the blood flows very close to the surface, that you must keep your head warm to keep the rest of your body warm. For headgear, a wool watchcap or balaclava, which comes down over the face like a mask, are the best. This gives you a warm layer next to your skin; plus, the insulated parka hood forms a layer to trap the warm air.

This, then, is the basic cold-weather clothing list. Obviously, many other choices are possible. Many x-c skiers prefer wearing flashy one- and two-piece ski suits that fit snugly and look great on people with streamlined figures. Warm-up suits, originally introduced by racers to x-c skiing, are also popular. In fact, they are seen so often on x-c skiers that they are rapidly becoming the official skiing uniform in some parts of North America. However, always determine the limitations of each type of clothing; consider versatility in keeping warm, as well as ease in dressing, movement, and undressing when answering the call of nature.

For casual skiing, the layering system is important because of the layers you need to add whenever you stop to keep from getting chilled. The layering system becomes essential, though, when you branch out from day trips, lodge visits, and resorts to winter camping on extended wilderness treks. Then, you can take no chances what-

soever with your clothing. It is all that stands between you and serious trouble.

We will discuss additional items of clothing, such as insulated parkas, footwear, and headwear in the camping section.

PART III
ON THE TRAIL

CHAPTER 6

CONDITIONING

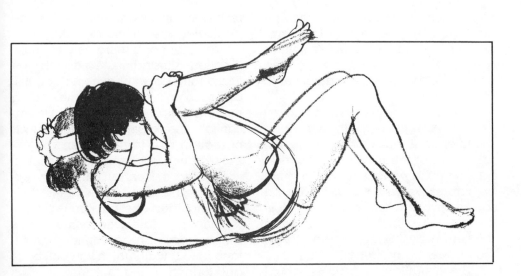

Unlike downhill skiing, which requires a special type of conditioning exercises, cross-country skiing closely parallels walking or running. Those who take up the sport tend to have the same vigor (or lack of same) they have for bare-ground sports such as strolling, walking, hiking, backpacking, jogging, and running.

As an example, hikers and backpackers are usually less interested in speed than joggers and runners; instead they tend to poke along, stopping to admire views, sniff flowers, or study landscapes. But joggers and runners are interested in miles and kilometers. Using this formula, hikers and backpackers are candidates for x-c skiing, joggers and runners for downhill skiing. This is an oversimplification, perhaps, but close to the mark.

In a sense, x-c skiing is a combination of several others sports—hiking or backpacking, skiing, camping, walking, and running. This makes it one of the most versatile and desirable forms of recreation, because you can tailor it to your own definition of outdoor fun.

Most people who take up x-c are already involved in a warm-weather activity that requires almost as much effort as skiing. So conditioning isn't always a major problem for the beginner. And since you have total control over how strenuous x-c skiing will be, you can ease into it at your own pace by learning in your backyard, a snow-covered golf course, a city park, or around the neighborhood. If you are a neighborhood stroller, you can now stroll on skis. Or if you feel your day is incomplete without running six or eight miles, you can accomplish the same goal on x-c skis. You will know from your own experience with other sports how hard you will want to work skiing.

You should obviously select companions whose attitudes toward mileage and exertion are the same as yours. It is easy for a group to become quite grouchy when a few of its members want to go for the equivalent of a stroll, while the others want to see how much distance they can cover in a single day.

You should be concerned primarily with strength in your legs, arms, shoulders, and back for x-c skiing. But this does not mean you will have to hang around weight rooms to build up impressive muscles. Most x-c ski racers have firm but not bulging muscles, much like runners, although skiers must be a bit more concerned with their upper body strength.

The conditioning process should be enjoyable, not a chore that is necessary for a weekend or week of fun. Try a variety of exercises: jogging, swimming, tennis, or handball. Doing something you enjoy is far superior to doing something that must merely be endured. If you enjoy the conditioning process, you'll probably enjoy x-c skiing more because it will simply be an extension of your other forms of exercise.

You may want to try one of several activities designed especially for x-c training. In New England, roller-skiing has been popular for many years. Roller-skis are x-c skis on wheels, so you can keep your skiing muscles and coordination at a peak throughout the year. Unfortunately, roller-skis have almost as many drawbacks as benefits. They are dangerous on roadways and sidewalks, so they have been banned in many places. A fall from roller-skis is almost always more painful than from x-c skis because you land on pavement rather than the soft, forgiving snow. But when used properly, roller-skis are as close as you can get to the real thing. However, they do represent an investment few but the dedicated are willing to make.

Another popular training exercise is called "ski-striding." To do this, you find a long slope, or even a steep hill, and race up it, using the same striding motions you would use on x-c skis. You can take the ski poles along for a touch of realism and to be certain you exercise your arms, back, and shoulders.

Some x-c skiers build their own exercise equipment to strengthen their arm, shoulder, and back muscles before the snow falls. One such device is simply strips of rubber inner tube attached to a wall, which you pull back and forth in poling motions.

These plus your normal physical-fitness program should suffice, unless you become involved in x-c racing, which is another story entirely.

Remember: If you are not in good condition, don't go skiing unless you will be content to ski at a slow pace. And if you take along friends who are not in good physical condition, be aware of the pace they need to make the outing both enjoyable and safe.

Here are some conditioning suggestions if you are a beginning skier and must admit to yourself that you aren't in top physical condition. If you have been inactive for a period of months or years, you should first check with your physician for his recommendations on your fitness program.

Running: This has been a national craze for some years and shows no signs of diminishing in popularity. As with all forms of exercise, consistency is extremely important. If you run one day, and then take the next four or five off, you've accomplished nothing.

Exercises: Again, once you start exercising, you must be committed to do it on a regular, daily basis. The exercise that is a form of punishment today will be a pleasant experience within a short time if you remain dedicated.

Following is a series of exercises designed to help you condition the muscles that you'll need for x-c skiing.

SKI TIP

If you are going to ride a chair lift to start your x-c skiing, remember that chair lifts are a common cause of cold feet because of the angle at which your legs dangle from the chair and because you are relatively immobile for several minutes in the cold. Isometric exercises should be done while on the lift, including alternately tensing and relaxing your leg muscles to force more circulation into your legs and feet.

First, try these tests to see what kind of condition you are in. Sit on the floor, with your legs straight out and together. If you can touch your toes and bring your head down to touch your knees, you're ahead of the class. Then, still sitting, spread your legs apart, keeping your knees straight. Place your fists on top of each other on the floor, and see if you can touch them with your forehead.

If you can't do either of these exercises, you need to work on your stretching. While doing stretching exercises, it is important to relax. It is equally important not to bounce, because this can cause muscles to tighten rather than loosen. While you are doing these exercises, don't force yourself. Bend or stretch as far as you can, then gradually push yourself without causing discomfort. Hold each stretch about 30 seconds and breathe deeply.

Another exercise, also performed while seated, is to put the soles of your feet flat against each other with your knees wide apart. Then cup your hands around your feet and push your head downward toward them. This strengthens your back and groin muscles.

After you have gotten back into reasonably good condition, then your muscles will be strong and flexible enough to do some twisting exercises. Sit on the floor with your right leg stretched out. Swing your left leg over your right and plant your left foot flat on the floor, outside your right leg. Lay your right arm against the outside of your left leg to hold it in place, then slowly twist your torso back and forth. Repeat the exercise with your legs reversed.

Stretch both legs together straight in front of you. Slowly extend your arms towards your feet until you can grasp your toes with your hands.

Sit on the floor with knees straight and legs spread. Place your fists on top of each other—then bend forward and touch them with your forehead.

With knees wide apart and soles of the feet against each other, cup hands around your feet and push your head downward toward your feet. This strengthens your back and groin muscles.

CONDITIONING

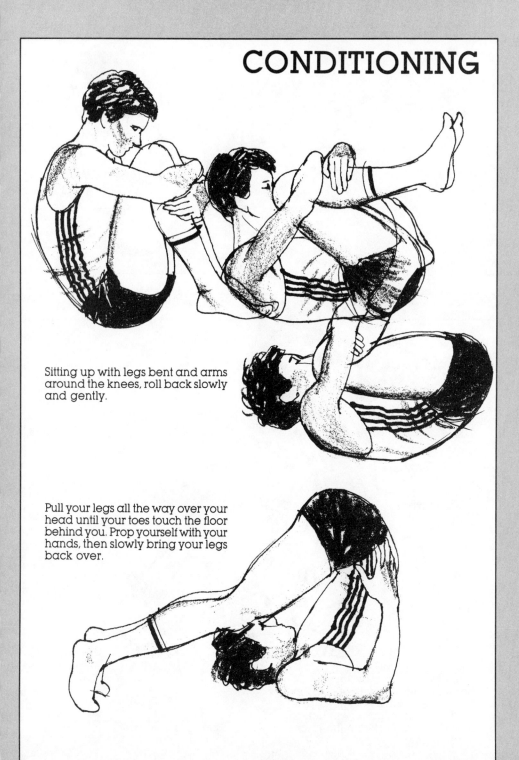

Sitting up with legs bent and arms around the knees, roll back slowly and gently.

Pull your legs all the way over your head until your toes touch the floor behind you. Prop yourself with your hands, then slowly bring your legs back over.

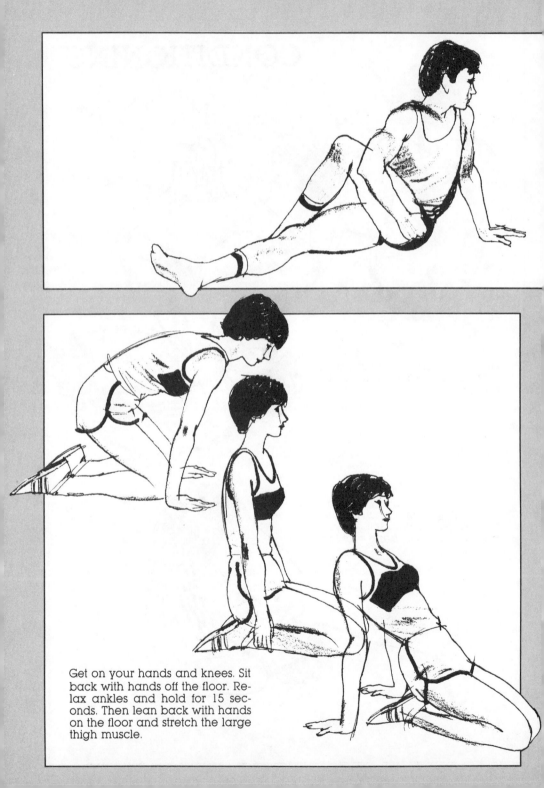

Get on your hands and knees. Sit
back with hands off the floor. Relax ankles and hold for 15 seconds. Then lean back with hands
on the floor and stretch the large
thigh muscle.

Left, sit on the floor with your right leg stretched out. Swing your left leg over your right and plant your left foot flat on the floor outside your right leg. You can lay your right arm against the outside of your left leg to hold it in place. Slowly twist your torso back and forth. Repeat the exercise with your legs reversed.

A good way to strengthen your arms is to perform a dipping exercise using your arms to lift your trunk. Sit on the floor next to a chair or bench with your hands on the edge. Then slowly lift yourself up and down, increasing the number as you build stamina.

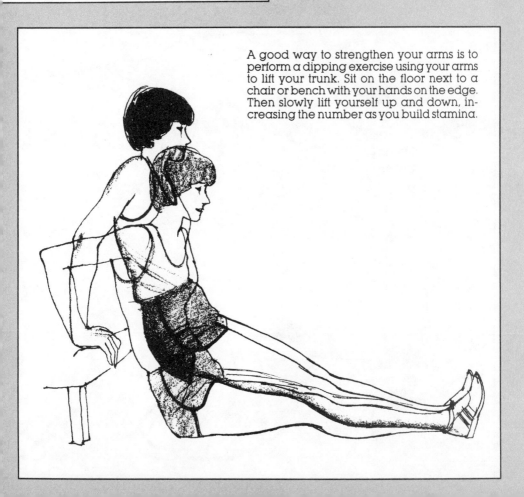

A

B

C

Left, these exercises strengthen back, neck and shoulder muscles.
A. Lie flat with fingers and toes pointed and try to make yourself grow an inch taller.
B. With your head flat, bring knees up to your chest. Now raise your head and shoulders, making your neck stretch.
C. With feet flat on the floor and hands behind your head, stretch neck and shoulder muscles **without** sitting-up.

This exercise requires a weight table, a piano bench, or a similar table. Lie on your stomach on the bench with your legs and hips on the bench and the rest of your body hanging over the end. Either hook your legs beneath the bench or have a companion sit on your feet. lace your fingers behind your head and raise your torso until it is level with the bench. Lower slowly to the floor again.

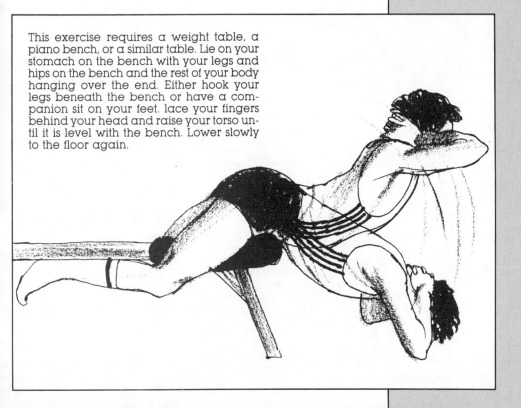

Stair jumping is a good exercise for simulating
the striding motions of skiing. Start on the bottom
stair with your left foot on the step and your right
poised in back of you. As you swing your right
foot forward, spring off from the ball of your foot
to land two or three steps up. When you spring
off the left foot, the left leg should be extended
to simulate the extension of a ski stride. Your right
leg should remain bent at the ankle and knee.
Try one jump at a time until you have mastered
the motion, and then gradually work up to a
series of a dozen or so jumps.

Some skiers prefer to do all their exercises as a series, or circuit. Find a suitable area where you can jog, do sit-ups, pull-ups, push-ups and arm bends. Do some warmup jogging for a few minutes, then go to your first station and do the exercises you have designated for that spot, jog to the next station for that exercise, and so on.

B

C

D

Run through these warm-up exercises just before hitting the trail

It is always a good idea to do some exercise after you have your skis on but before you start your touring or race. A. Plant your poles securely, then dip down into a deep telemark position. Hold it for at least a minute. Then reverse the stance. B. Stand, rest a mo-ment, then bend over to touch your toes. Hold that position for 60 seconds. C. Hold your poles in front of you with your arms stiff and outstretched. Slowly, take the poles back over your head and bring them down as far behind you as you can. D. To prepare yourself for the diagonal stride, take off your skis and plant your poles firmly in front of you. Then kick each leg front and rear, gradually exaggerating each kick as your legs loosen up.

A

CHAPTER 7

BASIC CROSS-COUNTRY TECHNIQUES

Ski instructors and manufacturers are fond of saying that if you can walk, you can cross-country ski. That is true, but don't expect to strap on a pair of skis and go soaring across the meadows and through the forests. It takes a bit of learning. Yet it is such an individual sport that you can do it at any speed or pace, any gait or style you want. It isn't as technical as many other sports, such as golf or fly-casting, so you can adapt it to your own wants and needs.

True, there are classic skiing techniques. Your instructor and this book will indicate those that have been proven the best for the majority of skiers. You don't have to lay down a perfect fish-spine set of tracks in order to herringbone up a hill, nor must you

resemble a modern-dance instructor to make an adequate telemark turn. But you may find skiing easier if you can perform these moves with style.

Take the advice offered here and use it as you see fit. The main thing about x-c skiing is to enjoy yourself; don't treat an outing as a ritualized dance before a critical audience. Personal enjoyment should be the major reason for taking up this or any other sport.

It is always wise to take a few lessons from a good instructor before starting any new sport, although you can always go out into a meadow or along an unused road and learn on your own. But if you take lessons, you'll save yourself some time, you'll probably fall less often, and you won't learn

PUSHING &
STRIDING

poor techniques you'll have to un-learn later.

Few pieces of recreational equipment are more awkward the first time they're used than a pair of skis. Down-hill skis feel strange; x-c skis feel worse. You'll probably tangle the skis the first time you try to take a step, because you're not accustomed to having something attached to your feet that is as long as you are tall. They flop around wildly; you start sliding and either tumble over without a trace of grace, or you bump into other skiers, buildings, or whatever else is unfortunate enough to be in your way.

All the while, experienced skiers are striding off gracefully into the forest or standing perfectly at ease like an advertisement in a ski magazine. You are certain that you are the clum-siest person who ever stepped onto a pair of skis.

Make it as easy on yourself as possible. Fortunately, most ski classes are conducted on flat terrain, such as a snow-covered parking lot, an open meadow, or a frozen lake covered with snow. Under these conditions, the learning process is much easier. Your skis won't be as likely to slip backward because of the wax or the machined bottoms of waxless skis.

Learning to be at least adequate on x-c skis isn't difficult. After your first weekend, you'll be surprised at how much easier your next weekend becomes. You'll make daily progress, as your afternoon skiing will be an improvement over your morning work-out.

The experienced downhill skier

may have a slight advantage over the complete novice, but the first time on x-c skis is awkward for everyone. The skis are lighter and longer, and they are less rigid than downhill skis; and since the heel isn't clamped to the skis, this presents another new sensation.

Find the flattest place you can to begin your learning: a playground, golf course, open meadow, or unused road. Strap on the skis and experiment with the way they move. Put your weight on one, then push ahead. Get the feel of the bottoms, waxed or waxless, and what it takes to keep you from sliding backward. Take a few tentative steps as though you were on slender snowshoes. Try simply walking with the skis on, rather than sliding them along, until you get accustomed to their feel. Learn as quickly as you can to use the "diagonal stride," the way you normally walk anyway.

SKI TIP

If you don't dig your skis in properly, you will take the proverbial "two steps forward and one step backward" when going uphill. Try curling your toes and pretend you are digging them into the snow when using the diagonal stride to go uphill. This will help you move your weight over your front ski where it is needed to set the ski and help it grip the snow. If you keep your weight equally balanced over both skis, you will slip backward.

SKATING ON SKIS

Find a slight incline and slide down it. You may fall or flail your arms and poles wildly like a character in a Saturday morning cartoon. Then either go back up the incline, making use of your waxed or waxless bottoms to go straight up, or sidestep, or even try the herringbone step to get back up the incline. The next trip down will be a little easier.

Try to avoid looking at the tips of your skis. You'll probably stare at them almost constantly at first because you won't have the control that comes with experience. But the sooner you learn to ski the way you walk—with only an occasional glance downward—the more you'll enjoy the landscape around you, and the more natural skiing will become.

You'll probably be out with other people on skis, perhaps some with experience. After you learn to stay on your feet for more than three or four awkward strides, play follow-the-leader with the more experienced ones. Imitate their movements.

This is now the best time to learn the proper way to fall.

FEAR OF FALLING

Everyone falls on skis—world champions and rank amateurs. It is a natural part of the sport and should be accepted as such. The trick, of course, is to learn to fall without injuring yourself, which involves relaxing to the proper degree and turning a fall into a collapse. Sometimes falls can even be graceful and merely a temporary inconvenience.

Keep these suggestions in mind:
- Try to land on your padding, either your clothing or the better padded parts of your body, such as your posterior, shoulders, and upper arms.
- Do not stick out your poles or your hands to lessen the impact, because you might injure yourself.
- Try to just sit down if possible, keeping your arms and knees up and out of the snow.
- If you can't avoid falling forward, try to fall on your side so that you land on your shoulder. Bring your arms close to your body and roll only to get your feet downhill. Then slide until you can stop.
- Always slide rather than roll, because rolling brings the flailing skis into the fall and creates the vivid—and often painful—eggbeater problem. Roll only to get your feet downhill, more or less together but not scissored. Stretch your body so that your elbows and knees won't dig into the snow.
- And above all, relax. Fall with a bounce rather than a bump.

Now that you've executed an elegant fall and are through rolling around and spluttering in the snow, you must get back onto your skis with the same aplomb. Here's how:
- It is easiest to get back up from the kneeling position, so shift around until your skis are at right angles to the steepest angle of descent (if you're on a hill).
- Kneel on your skis, plant your poles in front of you for balance, push up with your legs, and you're on your way again. This way, you use your leg muscles, which are stronger than your arm muscles.

Practice this while you're learning, because you'll need this skill as much as any other.

GOOD INSTRUCTORS

After you read all this material on how to perform the various maneuvers on x-c skis, don't make the mistake of thinking that you can go to a ski shop, rent a pair of skis, and then go striding across the meadows.

You can't learn to ski from a book. You've got to go out and do it, experiencing your allotted number of pratfalls, eggbeaters, and all the other humiliating events beginners must go through.

Thus, it is almost essential that you take some lessons from a professional. Your instructor will tell you essentially the same thing you've been reading here but has the advantage of being able to show you why these techniques work and why they are necessary.

FALLING—THEN GETTING UP WITH STYLE

You can learn x-c skiing only by doing it. And one of the best instructional methods is to play follow-the-leader across the snow, imitating the instructor stride for stride, turn for turn.

Unlike Alpine (downhill) skiing, if you live in an area with lots of snowfall, you can probably find a x-c school on the edge of town, at a municipal golf course, or somewhere within a few minutes' drive. Your local ski shop has the information, and many clubs and organizations such as the YMCA and YWCA offer x-c courses at reasonable rates.

Some activities are best taught by professionals. Just as you shouldn't teach your spouse or children to drive a car, so should you have them learn skiing from someone outside the family. Sometimes finding a good x-c ski instructor is almost as difficult as wading through promotional material in search of the perfect pair of skis and boots. Again, word-of-mouth is one of the best ways to find the proper instructor or school. Also consider those with long-standing reputations for instruction. Many lodges offer intensive x-c courses: during a weekend or winter vacation there you think and do nothing else but concentrate on x-c.

One of the dangers of dwelling at too much length on technique is that the sheer fun of the sport gets drowned in a sea of jargon. Too many people take recreation so seriously that they miss out on the pleasures because they become overly competitive and more concerned with how to do something than why to do it at all. In the beginning, x-c skiing was simply a way of getting around on the snow that also happened to be fun; to a large degree, it was brought to North America for practical uses. Unfortunately, its competitive aspects have made it a bit intimidating for some beginners who fear that they won't be as graceful on x-c skis as an Olympic contestant. This is a pity because, above all, x-c skiing is still what it was in the beginning—a means of getting about on the snow with ease.

In general, here are a few tips to consider when choosing an instructor, as suggested by the Ski Industries of America:

■ Good instructors start you from where you are; they find this out in advance by asking about your experience and your goals. Answer questions honestly, and don't pretend you are more (or less) experienced than you really are.

SKI TIP

There are two basic ways to keep your balance when skiing over varying terrain. One way is to crouch slightly at your knees, with your weight on the heel and ball of your foot. When the terrain suddenly steepens, rock forward slightly to keep up with the accelerating ski. When the hill flattens out, rock backward slightly. The other technique for keeping your balance when skiing over quickly changing terrain is to use a modified telemark position. This will make the slope transition seem less abrupt because the skis and body weight will be spread over a longer distance. Keep your poles at your side to function as outriggers when you plant them in the snow to maintain balance.

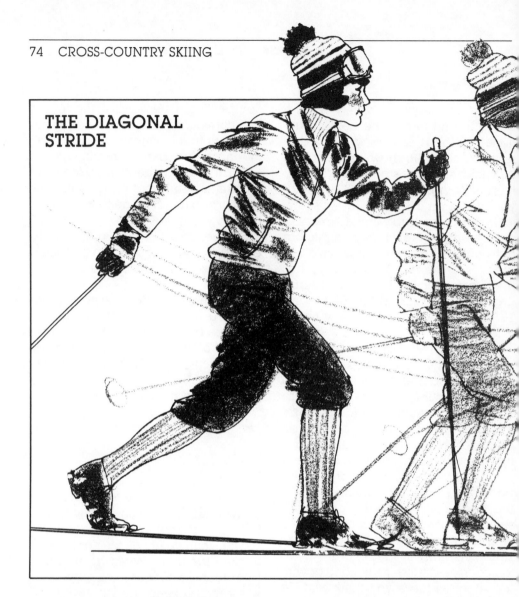

THE DIAGONAL STRIDE

- Good instructors know learners have anxieties; they understand and respect these anxieties, and calm them. Don't be afraid to admit you have them.
- Good instructors get you moving and performing right away, without burdening you with unnecessary theory, nomenclature, or body poses.
- Good instructors select achievement plateaus that provide pleasure and get to the first plateau quickly, but they do not let you progress to the next step until you have mastered the one before.

- Good instructors use demonstrations, mimicry, and touch the learner's body, using very little talking, explaining, or lecturing.
- Good instructors encourage learner self-discovery and know exercises for correcting errors.
- Good instructors know how far you can safely push yourself.
- Good instructors permit you to progress at your own pace, in your own style, to serve your own goals.

As you become more accomplished at getting yourself across the meadow and back without taking a

pratfall, you will gradually work your way from basic to more advanced maneuvers. Following are brief descriptions of these various common maneuvers.

THE DIAGONAL STRIDE

This is the basic method of moving along on your x-c skis. Its name comes from the fact that your arms and legs are used in a diagonally opposite manner. The left arm and the right leg

are swung forward at the same time, just like in walking. It keeps your balance intact and your body erect.

Do not use your poles as outriggers or training wheels. Learn to reach out and swing from the shoulders. Your arms should swing like pendulums from the shoulders in a natural motion, as in walking. Relax your hands to allow the larger shoulder muscles to give a more rhythmic and smoother poling motion.

Another method of insuring that you have the proper stride is to ski without poles. Since x-c skiing and ice

SNOW PLOW TURN

(Weight bias indicated by
darker shading)

skating use similar body motions, park your poles, put your hands behind your back, and slide one ski forward. As you slide the ski forward, push off with the other, then move on. Soon you will develop a rhythmic skating motion that feels natural; this will help you keep your weight balanced properly, slightly forward. This can be practiced on a slight downhill slope or on level ground.

DOWNHILL TURNS

Downhill x-c techniques have been getting more attention in recent years as skiers and manufacturers try to develop skis and techniques that give you the best of both Alpine and Nordic skiing. Lightweight and flexible x-c skis with metal edges for easy turns are becoming more and more popular among skiers who enjoy all types of skiing. There are also many varieties of bottoms for waxless skis that are being tried and introduced on the market.

The technology is changing and expanding so rapidly that this year's model is obsolete next year, so we will not attempt to go into any detail on

the various models. It is all very complicated for the beginner and bewildering even for the experienced and dedicated skier.

However, you should know the following turning techniques for x-c skis, no matter what kind you eventually own, because these turns form the basis of going down a hill after you've reached the top.

Snow plow: the basic turn is the snow plow, which is the first maneuver taught any skier. To execute this turn, point the tips of your skis together while your heels point outward. In other words, put your skis in a pigeon-toed

position; your weight should be evenly distributed on each ski, your body leaning slightly backward, your knees flexed, and your arms low with hands forward.

To turn left, lean on the right ski. To come out of the left turn, put your weight back on both skis. For a right turn, simply reverse the move.

After you have mastered the snow plow and feel comfortable with it, then you can move into the parallel turn and the traverse kick turn.

Traverse kick: the most common method of descending a gentle slope is with the traverse kick, a reverse of

STEP TURN

(Weight bias indicated by
darker shading)

the turning method used for going uphill. Keep your skis at about shoulder width apart, and point downhill at a comfortable angle and speed. When you want to turn back across the slope, shift most of your weight to the uphill ski. Step your skis slightly uphill until you stop. Then do a kick turn and proceed on downhill.

Step turn: step turns are used both for changing direction and controlling speed. For a sharp turn, keep making small steps with each ski until you are headed in the chosen direction. It is best to make these turns using only your feet and legs, rather than swinging the upper body. Stay relaxed and keep your knees bent slightly, using your poles for balance.

Stem turn: the stem turn, sometimes called the "stem christy," is just as easy to master as the step turn and is a second phase of the snow plow. First make the snow plow before you want to turn; place your weight on the downhill ski, which will make you turn in that direction, back across the face of the slope, your uphill ski slightly behind the downhill one. To straighten out, bring the skis parallel again, putting your weight on both evenly. Then, continue on your way.

STEM TURN

(Darker shade indicates weight bias)

Parallel turn: the parallel turn is similar to the stem turn in that you place your weight on the downhill ski, turn the uphill ski's tail outward (this is called stemming), and then shift your weight to that ski. Finally, bring the skis back together, parallel, and shift your weight to both skis again.

There are several variations of each of these turns, and after some practice, you will develop your own techniques, finding yourself combining some in order to make the turns you want. Again, given practice, these turns will become easier and more automatic the more you ski.

Telemark: the one turn that has gotten the most attention recently is the telemark. This is one of the most beautiful moves in all forms of skiing, but it is also one which will undoubtedly dump you a few times before you master it.

The telemark was named for the region of Norway where it was developed. A Norwegian ski jumper named Sondre Nordheim was credited with inventing the move during the 1860s, when he used it to complete his runouts after a jump. It became a turn technique that was handed down from skier to skier but was then ap-

PARALLEL TURN

KICK TURN

THE CLASSIC TELEMARK TURN

parently almost forgotten when Alpine skiing took over throughout most of Europe and North America. However, a few skiers remembered it and slowly reintroduced it in North America. Now it is one of the most popular maneuvers and generates much discussion among the more technical skiers.

The telemark isn't a simple maneuver to learn, so it isn't for the rank amateur or occasional skier who isn't in good condition. Like a complicated ice skating or ballet maneuver, it represents the peak of technique for many skiers.

Despite this debate—some skiers elevate this discussion about the telemark to impassioned controversy—the telemark is essentially a practical move for downhill skiing on the lightweight, flexible skis that must be treated with a great deal more gentleness than the stiff downhill skis. It is also the only turn performed on x-c skis that can't be done on downhill skis because it requires a loose heel rather than the unyielding bindings of downhill skis.

In essence, you transform a pair of skis into a single long ski. You can learn to perform it from either the diagonal stride or the snowplow.

From the stride, stretch one foot forward and steer that ski in the direction you want to go. Let the other ski swing around so that the tip is against the instep of your forward foot. While doing this, you will have to let your body sink very low on the skis so use your poles for balance. After the turn is completed, shift your weight back to the vertical position, pull the skis side-by-side again, and you're out of the telemark.

To make a telemark from a snow plow, which is easier for most skiers, slide the downhill ski back to a trailing position, with the tip against the instep of the forward ski; straighten it out until you're balanced on almost parallel skis, leaning into the turn.

It is very important to keep weight on the rear ski so that you won't be putting unnecessary weight and pressure on either leg; use both skis for the turn. While you're in the telemark position, your legs will be almost in a split, but you will need to keep your back straight. One way to force yourself to keep your back straight and your weight evenly distributed is to avoid looking down at your skis. This is difficult, especially when you're learning and need to see where your skis are. But keeping your head up and your eyes ahead will help ensure that you keep your back straight and weight distributed.

Other Downhill Techniques: There are other less technical ways to descend slopes, two involving the use of your poles. One of these is the pole drag. Place the poles between your legs and take your hands out of the straps. To prevent bending or breaking the poles, hold the tops with one hand and reach behind with the other, using it to apply pressure near the baskets.

You can also drag the poles beside you, keeping a precarious balance with your weight distributed between the poles and skis. You have to hold both poles in your hands on one or the other side.

A third method is not at all elegant but can be done with some aplomb. Simply ease downward on the skis until you are dragging the snow with the seat of your pants. Then you can gracefully slip the skis from beneath you and fall into the snow. While

learning, you'll get more practice in this maneuver than in any other means of stopping.

Uphill Techniques: Your skis are

WHEN IT'S TOO STEEP

Sometimes you will find slopes or mountainsides that are simply too steep and too rough for your ordinary waxed or waxless bottoms. But if you take off your skis and try to walk up, you'll create postholes in the snow and wear yourself out.

Here is where you'll need skins or climbing ropes that attach to the bottoms of your skis. Put them on to make the climb and then remove them after you reach the top; or leave them on if the terrain is equally rough on the way back down.

The skins used in climbing are not actually animal skins; they are pieces of fabric to which small hairs have been attached and arranged to face in the same direction, providing a gripping surface against the snow. Climbing skins are easily attached and removed.

Climbing ropes can be either purchased or made in the field; ropes that bought are usually made of one-fourth inch rope, while those that are homemade are made of nylon rope. Climbing ropes are woven and tied around the skis using figure eight knots underneath and overhand knots on top.

POLE-DRAGGING SLOWS YOUR DESCENT

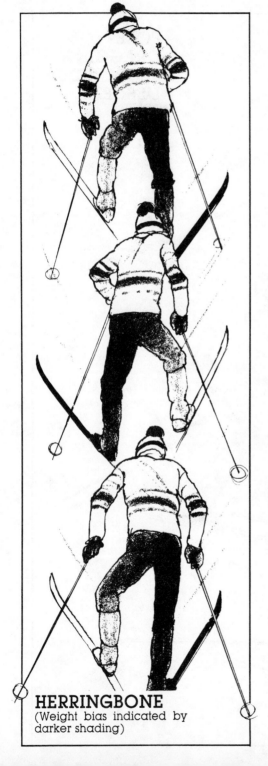

HERRINGBONE
(Weight bias indicated by darker shading)

designed to go up slight inclines when you shorten your normal strides into more brisk, choppy strides, like when you take shorter steps walking uphill than you do on flat ground. However, on x-c skis, you will expend more effort as you slap down one ski to get a grip and plant the next one while your weight is still near the vertical line.

When you come to hills that are too steep for your skis to get a good grip, use either of two basic steps: the herringbone or the sidestep. Both look ungainly when you're just learning, but they're easy to master and both permit you to continue on your way with only a slight decrease in speed.

Herringbone: the herringbone is the first method beyond striding. You turn the tips of the skis outward, something like Charlie Chaplin's famous spraddle step, and dig the inside edge of each ski into the snow. You'll probably rap your ankle or calf with the rear of the skis a few times before the

---

SKI TIP

As your skiing progresses, you will learn the double pole technique for flat ground and gentle downhill skiing. Be aware of a mistake that is often made: The tendency is to sit down when pushing against the poles. This technique creates an up-and-down motion that expends too much of your energy and accomplishes nothing. Instead, lean forward; then push backward with the poles angled toward the rear and not planted straight up and down.

SIDE STEP

(Darker shade indicates weight bias)

step becomes comfortable, but when it does, you will quickly shift from the normal stride into the herringbone without thinking.

Side Step: the side step is simply what it name implies. You turn at a right angle to the hill and begin stepping sideways up the hill, turning your knees slightly toward the slope to give the edges of your skis a good purchase. Some skiers do this with another purpose in mind—to pack down

SKI TIP

To improve your uphill skiing on gentle slopes, "put your best foot forward." Thrust the gliding ski far ahead of you so that your foot is ahead of your knee. This helps keep your kick under you and not behind where it can cause you to slip.

HOW TO PASS

When passing a skier who has stopped beside the track, start with a vigorous push-off in the direction desired. Let your outside ski pass over both grooves of the main track before bringing your inside ski into place; finally, bring your outside ski into the track before continuing on. When you approach a slow skier or a group of skiers on a double track, pass easily and safely by skating from one set of tracks to the other.

a hillside for a pleasant downhill run after they've reached the top.

Traverse Turn: if a hill is particularly steep and long, you can reduce the climbing effort by making a traverse route, zig-zagging back and forth across the face of the slope so that you are still climbing but not so vertically. When you reach the end of a traverse and want to tack back in the other direction, you will have to make a kick turn.

Put your pole on the uphill side, just below where the track of your next traverse will be. Then put all your weight on the downhill ski and swing the uphill ski around to the new direction. Shift your weight to that ski, swing the other one around to parallel the uphill ski, and you're aimed in the direction you want to go.

You can check your herringbone and side-step technique by looking backward at your tracks. The herringbone track should look as though it were an impression made by the spine of a giant fish. A side-step track should be no wider than the length of your skis.

Both steps, as well as the kick turn, can be practiced on flat terrain so you get the feel of the methods before tackling an incline.

Downhill Turns: downhill x-c techniques have gotten more attention in recent years, as skiers and manufacturers have improved both skis and techniques to give you the best of both Alpine and Nordic skiing. Lightweight and flexible skis with metal edges for easy turns are becoming more popular, because they help bridge the gap between the two kinds of skiing. Each season, many varieties of waxless skis are introduced that serve both skiing needs better and better.

The technology is changing and expanding so rapidly that this year's sophisticated model is outdated next year, so no attempt will be made to go into great detail on the various models that were new when this was written. It is all quite complicated for the beginner, and many of the high performance skis are not really appropriate for learning anyway.

However, you should master the turning techniques described and illustrated, no matter what kind of x-c skis you eventually own. These moves form the basis of getting down a hill . . . enjoyably . . . after you've reached the top.

CHAPTER 8

FINDING YOUR WAY

Unless you are going on a winter expedition into unfamiliar land, you will do most of your cross-country skiing and winter camping in places that you've hiked and camped during the summer months. Most x-c skiers stick to well-defined trails and equipment.

However, you may take a trip that begins modestly, but when the fine weather holds up and everyone in the group is able to cover more miles than anticipated, you may be tempted to stretch your trip a few miles going over a low divide into the next basin and returning to the car by an alternate route.

Thus, you need to to carry topographical maps and a compass on all outings. In almost any group of more than two, there will be at least one who feels so invigorated by the weather and scenery that he will insist on pushing on and extending the trip. If you have the navigational equipment and the skills to use it, and your food supply is adequate, why not?

TOPOGRAPHICAL MAPS

Topographical maps are the standard for outdoorsmen all over North America. The only way to become accustomed to them is to use them in the outdoors. Nothing replaces practical applications of the maps, and while you can pore over

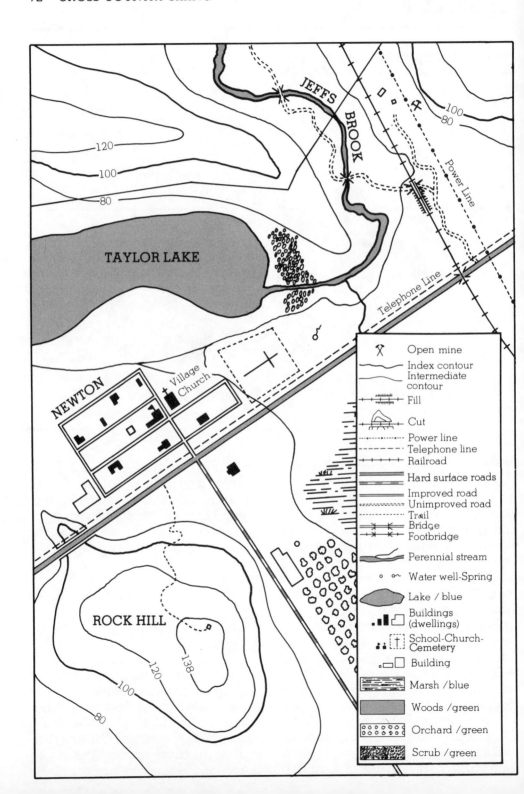

	Open mine
	Index contour
	Intermediate contour
	Fill
	Cut
	Power line
	Telephone line
	Railroad
	Hard surface roads
	Improved road
	Unimproved road
	Trail
	Bridge
	Footbridge
	Perennial stream
	Water well-Spring
	Lake / blue
	Buildings (dwellings)
	School-Church-Cemetery
	Building
	Marsh / blue
	Woods / green
	Orchard / green
	Scrub / green

them for hours at home to select potential campgrounds or skiing trails, still you must consult them in the actual terrain to learn how to read them at a glance.

These "topo" maps are color-coded. Features such as buildings, roads, railroads, mines, windmills, churches, and schools are all printed in black. Water features are in blue. Vegetation is in green, and all the elevation indicators such as contour lines, altitude markings and benchmarks are in brown.

Remember, though, that water will be ice and perhaps covered with snow in the winter; some vegetation, such as marshes, will also be covered.

Nearly all maps have detailed instructions printed on them along with a key to the symbols.

The standard map for outdoor enthusiasts is on the scale of 1:24,000, which means one unit on the map (this may be a kilometer or a mile or whatever has been chosen and noted) equals 24,000 of the same units in actuality. For example, a mountain that is shown on the map to be no larger than a pencil eraser will actually be 24,000 times as large.

Each topo map also shows the declination correction factor, which is vital in using your compass.

Topo maps are available at nearly every major outdoor supply store, at map stores, and by mail order from the U.S. Geological Survey. If you know the specific map or maps you need by their quadrangle names, fine. But it is best to write and ask for an index map, which shows the whole United States, and then breaks it down into increasingly small portions, or quadrangles, so you can order exactly what you need.

Almost identical maps are available for all of Canada through the Geological Survey of Canada.

It is essential to keep topo maps up to date. National Forest roads are continually being built, obliterated, or extended. Buildings shown on maps burn or vanish. New ones are built. New landmarks, such as microwave towers and power transmission lines, are built. So it is best to order your topo maps directly from the USGS if possible, since outdoor stores might have an older edition that hasn't sold out.

Topographical maps are available at nearly every outdoor supply store, or by writing:

United States, East of the Mississippi:
    Distribution Section
    USGS
    Washington, D.C. 20204

United States, West of the Mississippi:
    Distribution Section
    USGS
    Federal Center
    Denver, CO 80225

Canada, all parts:
    Canada Map Office
    Department of Energy, Mines
    and Resources
    615 Booth Street
    Ottawa, Canada K1A 0E9

THE COMPASS

The compass is a needle magnetized on one end and balanced on a pin so it can swing freely. The magnetized end will always point toward the Magnetic North Pole unless it is deflected by local ore deposits (a rare occurrence) or metallic objects you are carrying.

The magnetized needle is mounted above a dial that shows all the major directions, and often is marked off in the 360 degrees of a circle as well. Covering most compasses is a plastic plate that can be turned, and it is printed with an arrow marked "north".

A compass does not point toward the North Pole. It points toward the Magnetic North Pole, which is approximately 1,000 miles from the North Pole in northern Canada. This magnetic field tends to wander slightly, but not enough to make a lot of difference in your direction finding. At the most, it wanders only a degree.

All maps are based on the North and South poles. They are the only constants from which cartographers can operate with total accuracy. This means that your compass and the maps you carry do not match: Whereas the longitude lines on the map point north, your compass will point a few degrees in another direction, toward magnetic north.

The angle of difference between the North Pole and the Magnetic North Pole on your compass is called the "declination." This varies in different parts of North America, and all U.S. and Canadian Geological Survey

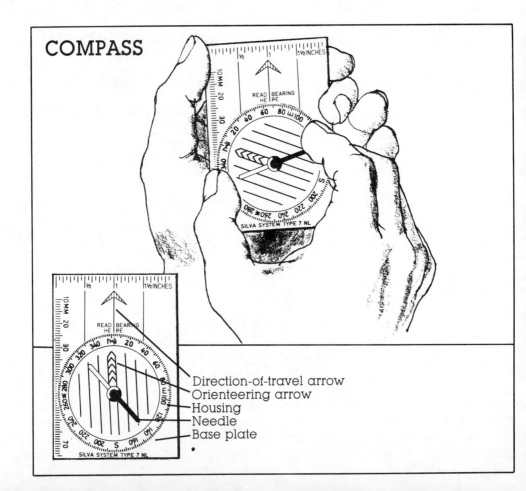

COMPASS

Direction-of-travel arrow
Orienteering arrow
Housing
Needle
Base plate

TRAIL MARKING SYSTEM

A standard trail-marking system has been initiated nationwide for Nordic ski areas.

maps have the angle of declination printed on them.

This is where the plastic covers of the best compasses are needed. When you plan to use your compass on a trip, you must first consult the map of the area you will be traveling and find the angle or degrees of declination on it. Then you hold the compass with the arrow pointing to north on the dial, count the degrees of declination in the direction away from true north, and turn the upper dial to that point. Thus, the printed arrow will always point to the North Pole while the magnetized needle points to magnetic north.

This is the basis of all navigation by map and compass. The rest is applied mathematics and is relatively simple, provided you learn navigation in easy stages. If you think you may need to use a combination of map and compass on a trip, it is vital that you practice with them before the trip, and that practice should be thorough and often enough so that you are as

comfortable with the compass as you are with street maps.

As you become more adept at using the compass and maps, you may want to invest in more complex compasses. There are several different kinds available, each with its own uses. Of the five basic types, the **fixed-dial** compass has already been described. There's also the **lensatic** compass, equipped with a dial that pivots beneath the magnetized needle and has an azimuth scale that also is adjustable.

The **cruiser**, designed for forestry engineers and timber cruisers, has a dial with the degrees printed counterclockwise. It is of little use for recreationist.

The **sighting** compass is a sophisticated and highly accurate hand-held compass with a sighting lens in the case that magnifies the dial to within one-half-degree readings. They are useful for canoeists who want to maintain a totally accurate course, and for other similar uses.

The **orienteering** compass is a sophisticated design that can be lain on maps for plotting routes. It has a transparent plastic plate for a base that is marked on one side with the map scale in millimeters; another side has the scale in inches.

CHAPTER 9

FIRST AID FOR COMMON INURIES

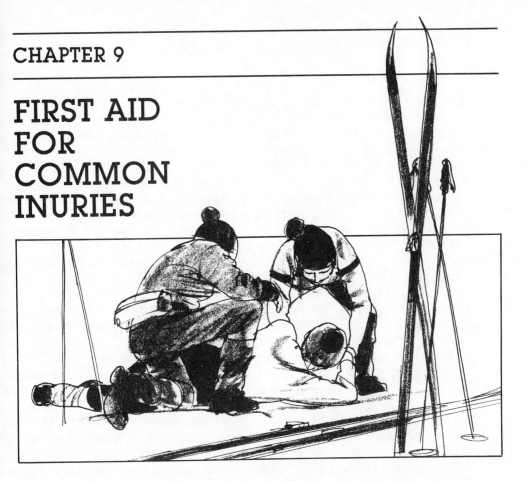

You face the same kind of injuries in winter camping as you do in summer camping, with the added dimension of problems caused by cold. Campers pick up hot pots, burn themselves on stove parts, and scald their legs by spilling hot drinks. They cut their fingers on knives and sharp can lids. They get headaches, stomach aches, sprained ankles, and sometimes worse.

Good physical conditioning and common sense will prevent most of these injuries, and since most winter campers are better skilled in the outdoors than summer campers, the incidence of injury is considerably less. However, accidents happen to the most experienced outdoors people, and you should be prepared for these common injuries.

The injuries can be broken down into those that occur due to the cold, those that are common in camp, and those that are related to skiing.

Cold-related injuries include frostbite, freezing, and hypothermia. Avalanches will be discussed in a separate chapter.

First, we need a discussion on the physiology of cold.

KEEPING WARM

We have become so accustomed to relying on external heat sources to stay warm in the winter that we tend to forget what factors are at work in our bodies—and outside them—that have a profound effect on our ability to stay warm outdoors.

The catch words are conduction, radiation, convection and evaporation. Perhaps the best way to explain these terms is to give an illustration.

Suppose you take a break and sit on a rock or on the snow. Unless you're sitting on insulation, such as a closed-cell foam pad, you will lose heat from your body to the cold object on which you're sitting. This is called **conduction.**

Then you unzip your parka, and the breeze blows away some of the warm air trapped inside. This is called **convection.**

Your face will lose some of your body heat, because it is the only part of your body exposed. This is called **radiation.**

If you've been sweating while skiing, the cold air will dry your body and wet clothing through the other form of heat loss, **evaporation.**

At this point, the only thing protecting you against freezing to death is the heat your body produces naturally from its fuel (food) and your body's metabolism, which consumes excess fuel in the form of fats.

Thus, it is important to understand how the body functions in a cold, hostile environment and to be aware of ways to retain body heat around the core areas.

Core areas are the parts of the body that contain the major organs—the brain, heart, and lungs. If you protect these areas properly, you won't be bothered by the cold. Your hands, arms, feet, and legs can drop a few degrees in temperature and cause no ill affects, provided of course they don't freeze. But a drop of one or two degrees in the temperature of the brain, heart, or lungs has a dramatic and dangerous effect.

The body has its own defense mechanisms over which we have little control. As soon as the major organs begin cooling, the body immediately reacts to protect them by cutting down the circulation of warm blood to the extremities; the body is willing to sacrifice them to save the major organs. Thus, the feet and hands are frostbitten first.

There's an old adage which says, "If your feet are cold, put on a hat." This expresses a simple truth about your body's protective mechanisms. In most cases, when your feet start getting cold it is because the blood supply is being restricted in order to pump more to the scalp, where too much heat is escaping. Put on a warm hat and soon the blood will circulate normally to the feet.

Another major factor in cold survival is to keep enough liquids in the body. Too often we associate dehydration with hot weather, yet it is as much a problem in the winter. We lose enormous amounts of body liquids through the simple process of breathing; this loss increases sharply with gains in elevation.

SKI TIP

A specialist in cold-weather research has determined that almost all mammals automatically reduce the blood supply to their extremities when their face is exposed to wet temperatures below 70° F. Thus, keep your face and head protected and you will protect your hands and feet, as well.

Dehydration is a major contributor to frostbite and hypothermia, because it affects the circulatory system by drawing moisture from the blood as it passes through the lungs. The blood thickens and doesn't feed the smaller capillaries, slowing overall circulation.

At the same time, heat is lost through the breathing process, and unless your body has a sufficient supply of moisture, hypothermia can result as well as freezing. It is one of nature's small ironies that you can be skiing all day on tons of water in the form of snow, yet be suffering from dehydration, just like a sailor without fresh water at sea.

Snow itself is a poor substitute for water. It steals body heat when you place it in your mouth and takes so much stove fuel to melt that it should not be depended upon for drinking water. If you are camping away from a stream, you'll need to keep a pan of water near heat at all times, adding snow frequently in order to melt enough for your use.

In addition to keeping your body furnace warm and filled with liquids, you also need a steady supply of fuel. Your blood needs its primary food, sugar, which is produced from regular foods as well as quick-energy foods such as candy, starches, and dried fruits. Thus, there is a need for what has become known as "trail food"— candy, nuts, raisins, and fruits—to keep your body fueled with food that is quickly turned into blood sugar. Food that is more difficult to digest, or at least slower to digest, such as fats and proteins, are good for dinners; they will keep you warm throughout the night as they are slowly digested and turned into body fuel.

TREATING FROSTBITE

Frostbite occurs most often on skiers' cheeks when they do not wear face masks. The toes are the next most vulnerable area, followed by the fingers. The cheeks are the easiest to spot, because frostbite creates a telltale white or whitish-yellow patch. Groups of skiers out in frigid conditions should check each others' cheeks frequently for these signs.

Treatment for frostbite is relatively simple in most cases. Find shelter and place the warm palm of your hand against the spot until normal color returns. Then call it a day, because once a patch of skin has been frostbitten, the tissues are weakened and will easily frostbite again.

You may not know when your cheek has been frostbitten, because your face will already be numb from the cold, so it is important that you use the buddy system to watch out for each

SKI TIP

If you have problems with cold feet, consider how you store your boots. Many skiers just toss their boots into the car trunk and bring them out at the ski area to put them on cold. Even if you take your boots out of the trunk and warm them by the car heater, they will probably have moisture condensed in them. Keep your boots in the car with you all the time and put them on while they're warm and dry.

Place your warm hand on your frostbitten cheek until normal color returns

other. However, you will know when the circulation is restored to the damaged area due to the sharp, tingling caused by the blood reentering the damaged tissue. Some outdoorsmen call this sensation the "northern hurt dance," because it can be quite painful.

Do not rub the frostbitten spot, because you will probably damage the tissue further. Also, contrary to medical practices of the past, do not rub snow on frostbite; that will only make it worse and the granules of the snow may tear the tender skin.

The extremities, particularly the feet and toes, are prone to frostbite. Restoring feeling to the hands is quite easy in most cases; tuck them under your armpits to warm them enough for circulation to return. But when your feet are frostbitten while you're out in the field, you must rely on the good

graces of a friend who will let you tuck your bare and frigid feet against his tender, warm belly. As Bob Cary wrote, this is when you find out who your friends really are.

It is best to cover the affected area to prevent further frostbite; then go back to the camp or lodge to treat the injury, particularly if it is more serious than a small patch on a cheek. Unless the entire body is warm, its natural defense mechanisms will continue restricting the blood supply to the surface areas—especially the frostbitten area—and the injury will be easily repeated.

In the case of a frozen foot, it is better for the victim to walk several hours until the whole body can be rewarmed than to warm only the frozen area while the rest of the body remains cold.

Immersion in warm water is the

best way to rewarm a frozen foot. The water should be only sightly warmer than the normal body temperature; from 100° F to 108° F is best. If the water is too uncomfortable to hold your hand in, it is too hot for the victim's frozen flesh.

A frostbite-related injury occurs when bare skin makes contact with a piece of frozen metal; the skin will stick to the metal, sometimes tearing when it is removed. The result is similar to a burn, complete with blister. Treat the injury by keeping it clean, dry, and covered with a gauze bandage.

HYPOTHERMIA

New definitions of hypothermia continue to be offered, because it is such a serious problem. Yet, it is very difficult to self-diagnose. New ways are constantly being sought to convince recreationists of its dangerous nature and that it can move quickly to an advanced stage before the victim is aware that there is a problem.

Essentially, hypothermia is a condition in which the body suffers heat loss that it cannot replace without using an outside source of heat.

Nearly everyone who has traveled outdoors has suffered from the first stage of hypothermia, which is severe shivering. We put on a warmer coat, turn up the furnace thermostat, stoke up the campfire, exercise by jogging in place, crawl into a sleeping bag, and drink hot drinks—all of which assist the body in regaining its normal temperature.

Although our bodies are incredibly rugged and can withstand fatigue, temperature extremes, and severe injuries, still, when the delicate temperature balance is upset, we are in immediate trouble. A drop of one or two degrees in the temperature of our blood is extremely dangerous.

Hypothermia was formerly called "exposure," but as it became better understood and its stages were identified, the more exact definition came into use.

As with most outdoor hazards, the

Two items you do not need to use in cold weather are alcohol and tobacco. Alcohol is what is known as a **peripheral vasodilator**. It causes blood vessels, particularly those close to the skin, to remain open even when the body's thermostatic system sends out signals to close down. This is what causes the flushed feeling and appearance in the face; blood rushes in to warm the face, but in the process it is cooled by the outside temperature so cooled blood returns back to the heart. Alcohol also reduces shivering, which is the first symptom of hypothermia, thus ignoring the body's automatic effort to create muscle heat and overcome the cold.

Tobacco has the opposite effect. It is a **peripheral vasoconstrictor** and tightens the small blood vessels, but not when the body's thermostat wants it to. Consequently, tobacco can shut down the blood vessels and cause frostbite when the body would ordinarily compensate on its own and prevent the condition.

HYPOTHERMIA

Hypothermia victims go through four stages of the condition unless treated promptly and properly.

Shivering

Uncontrolled, violent shivering, and difficulty with speech

Erratic movements, stiff muscles, and inability to think clearly

Irrational behavior, unconsciousness, and death

It is essential to treat the hypothermia victim quickly.

Get the victim warm and into dry clothing.

Stoke up a big fire.

Feed the victim hot drinks.

Walk the victim around to force his or her body to rebuild its own heat sources.

Once the danger is past, keep the victim warm and comfortable.

symptoms and treatment of hypothermia are relatively simple. But you have to know them thoroughly to recognize the dangers and to treat them properly.

The primary stage of hypothermia is tiredness and prolonged shivering, which may be caused by wetness, cold, or wind. If these symptoms are not treated quickly, the next stages of hypothermia can follow rapidly. The victim becomes disoriented; he may stumble and babble incoherently. Next comes coma, followed by death.

The treatment of primary hypothermia is to stop when the signs occur: Get out of the wind or wet, and build a shelter and a fire; get the victim warm and dry; have him drink something warm and eat quick-energy food such as candy. Help the body restore its own heat source, too, by making the victim move about, jog in place, and swing his arms, all of which will help restore circulation and get warm blood flowing back to the extremities, as well as to the brain.

Restoring the circulation of blood is essential, because once bloodflow has been curtailed in the primary stages, it deteriorates rapidly. The shivering in primary hypothermia is the body's automatic attempt to force muscles to move so as to keep the blood flowing throughout the body. When this does not work because of continuing development of hypothermia, the blood supply to the extremities is reduced as the body's defense mechanisms act to keep the warm blood close to the heart, lungs, and other core organs. But as this happens, the blood supply to the head and brain is restricted because the neck, face, and scalp are chilled and the blood vessels in them are constricted.

When treating a hypothermia victim in the field, if nothing else works, make a cocoon of all clothing available; then strip off your own clothing and get into the cocoon with the victim. Try to rewarm the victim with the heat from your own body. However, this isn't always necessary, let alone practical; besides, you are placing yourself in danger of hypothermia, too, so be careful.

It is important to use the buddy system to watch out for each other, not only for frostbite but also for behavioral changes, such as erratic movement and a drop in coordination and response. Hypothermia victims can self-diagnose the primary stage of uncontrollable shivering, but after that, their judgment is too impaired to make any further decisions for themselves. It is up to you, the buddy, to decide if you should stop, make shelter, and begin treatment.

Remember: Once the process starts, the body can no longer correct itself without sources of external heat. Taking in fuel in the form of high-energy foods provides internal heat. If the victim has on wet clothes, they must be removed and replaced with dry clothing immediately. If you have a campfire, try to prewarm the clothes before putting them on the victim. Hot water bottles or any such substitute will help restore body warmth.

SKI TIP

Keep your water bottle on a thong around your neck and beneath your parka so it won't freeze while you're traveling.

If diagnosed early enough, the condition can be treated quickly and the victim will be fine after being warmed and fed. But since the body has been through a trauma, the victim should not try to pretend that nothing has happened and continue at a fast pace. The remainder of the day should be spent resting and letting the body recover from the shock.

Death due to hypothermia has been decreasing during the past decade, due to the intensive educational program that has been carried out by outdoor organizations, the medical profession, and equipment manufacturers. Also, outdoor clothing has improved so much over the years that it, too, has been a factor in preventing hypothermia.

So remember the causes—wet, cold, wind—and the early signals—fatigue, prolonged shivering. Then, know the treatment—stop, get shelter, build a fire, get warm and dry, drink and eat, exercise.

SPRAINS

Sprains are almost taken for granted by downhill skiers who are out on the slopes frequently. Sprains are also relatively common among x-c skiers, especially ankle sprains caused when the body tries to go one direction and the skis insist on going another. Other sprains do occur, of course, including knee, finger, and wrist injuries.

The basic treatment for sprains is to immobilize the joint, preventing further damage to the ligaments, tendons, and tissues. A Coba or Ace bandage can be used to immobilize

an ankle by tying it on over the boot. Or nylon cord can be used if bandages aren't available. Since swelling always occurs, it is best not to remove the boot; it probably won't fit back on and the victim will need the boot to avoid frostbite or freezing. At the same time, the swelling inside the boot will reduce circulation, which is an invitation to frostbite, too. The foot and ankle should be immobilized with a bandage and wrapped with a plastic bag or stuff sack to retain as much warmth as possible. Then get back to the camp or lodge as soon as possible.

Once you are back to permanent shelter, the boot can be removed and the swelling can be treated with cold packs made of snow or ice. These cold applications should be brief, and the ankle should be kept warm in between them.

A sprained wrist or finger is easier to treat because the victim will still be mobile. Treat the injury with cold packs to reduce the immediate swelling; then the injury can be immobilized and wrapped for warmth until you return to camp or leave for a doctor's office.

DISLOCATIONS

These are a very painful injury, sometimes more so than sprains or broken bones, and should be treated in the same way as a sprain; immobilize the joint with a splint or sling and evacuate the victim. Sometimes a dislocated finger can be pulled back into place by a knowledgeable companion but it is work best left to a physician. Don't even consider trying to replace a dislocated shoulder unless you can legally hang out your M.D. shingle.

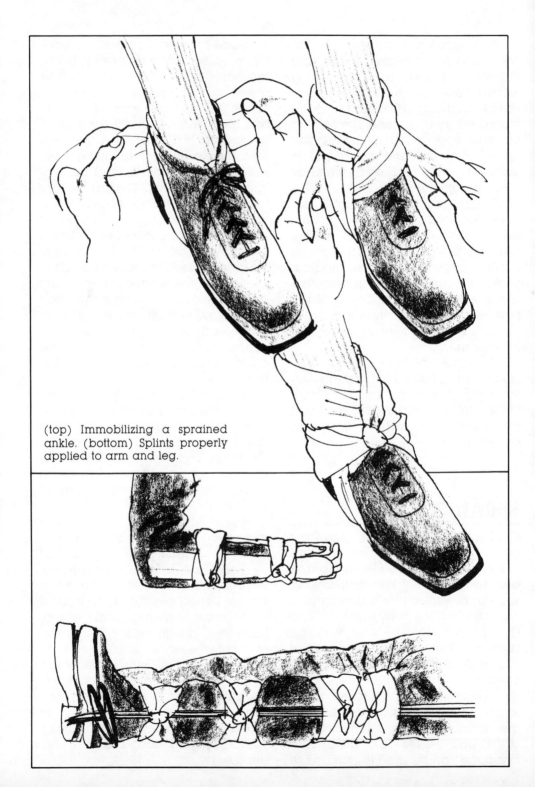

(top) Immobilizing a sprained ankle. (bottom) Splints properly applied to arm and leg.

BROKEN BONES

Sometimes a broken ankle or leg will be confused with a bad sprain. The victim will usually hear the bone break, but this isn't always the case, and not all breaks show as a lump with discoloration against the skin. Sprains and breaks should be treated in essentially the same way: Immobilize the limb, apply cold packs to reduce the swelling, and evacuate the victim for medical help.

If an ankle or leg is broken, the victim cannot be expected to get out of the area on his own. He must be transported, either by sled, by a skid made of skis, or by evacuation through search-and-rescue units. In the summer when there is bare ground, victims of broken ankles or shins can sometimes be evacuated under their own power with the help of companions. But in the winter, snow adds the danger of falling and compounding the injury, so evacuation is more difficult.

If you don't have the means of building a sled or skid with you, build a good shelter for the victim, providing food, a fire, and plenty of warm clothing to offset the effects of shock. Then go for help. This is one of the best arguments for traveling in parties of three or more on x-c ski outings. You can have one person stay with the victim while the third goes for help.

Broken bones should be splinted. Splints can be made from ski poles in an emergency, but then you can't use your poles when getting the victim out. Pieces of cardboard boxes are excellent for this purpose, as are sticks of wood. Use a sleeping bag or clothing to make the splint well-padded.

In the case of a compound frac-

ture where the bone penetrates the skin, slit the clothing away and check for bleeding. If necessary, stop the bleeding and then cover the wound with gauze pads; build the splint on the outside of the clothing.

If the victim has two broken legs, you can splint both legs together, placing padding in between them; then slip the victim's legs into a sleeping bag when transporting.

In all cases, keep the victim as warm as possible. Bundle him into a sleeping bag, add extra warm clothing, and if it is extremely cold, be sure his face is covered with a face mask or scarf. The victim's extremities will be more susceptible to the cold because shock will reduce the flow of blood to the extremities, so bundle up the hands and feet.

CUTS

A minor cut should be cleaned and covered with a bandaid. A deeper cut should be cleaned and the sides of the incision held together with a butterfly bandaid. Don't be surprised if you suddenly see blood on something you've handled without knowing your hand is cut because your hands will be numbed by the cold and you won't feel the cut occur.

Puncture wounds sometimes occur when two people on skis get too close together and suddenly a pole tip rips into a companion's leg. In this case, clean the puncture with warm water and the mildest soap you have in camp, and then cover it with a sterile bandage. Change the bandage frequently and watch for signs of infection. If this occurs, leave for the nearest doctor. If the puncture wound

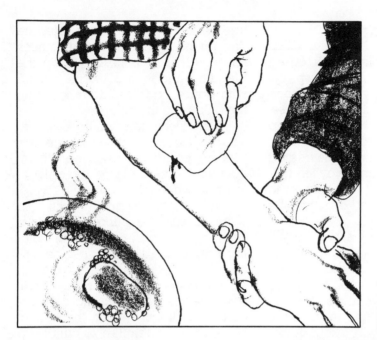

Cleanse wound with mild soap and water—then apply sterile bandage

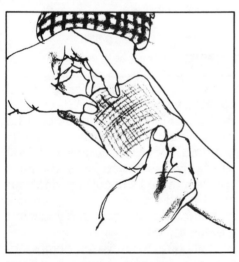

is a bad one, leave immediately, without waiting for signs of infection.

BURNS

The first thing to do when you've burned yourself is to plunge the burned area into snow and leave it there for awhile. Then dry it carefully to avoid damaging the tissue further, and wrap it with a dry bandage. If a blister develops, leave it alone to avoid the possibility of infection.

If the burn is severe, such as from spilled stove fuel or even a tent burning, and clothing is stuck to the wound, cover the area with a sterile bandage and treat the victim for shock by keeping him warm and drinking warm liquids. Evacuate as soon as possible. Do not try to remove the clothing on the burned area and do not apply ointments or any other liquid.

OTHER WINTER AILMENTS

Headaches are relatively common in the winter and can be caused by over-exertion, eye strain, and the effect of cold air on your sinuses. Aspirin and rest is the usual treatment.

Stomach aches are commonly caused by food, although the likelihood of spoiled food is lessened in the cold weather. Other causes may include allergies to certain foods, eating snow, overindulgence of certain foods

SNOW BLINDNESS

The best treatment for snow blindness, of course, is to avoid it. Snow blindness can occur quite rapidly on lightly overcast days, so you should always wear sunglasses. But if it does occur, you'll feel it quickly because your eyes will feel gritty, they will burn and water a lot, and if the burn is severe, they will swell shut.

The treatment is to keep the victim out of the sunlight and cover his eyes, alternating with cold compresses and clean bandages, until the condition disappears.

or drinks, or even not enough food and drink.

Asphyxia is more common in recreational vehicles than in tent camping, but if your tent doesn't have proper ventilation, a stove, lantern, or heater is too dangerous to use inside for even a few minutes. The common backpacking tents, which are used on most x-c ski trips, are designed to have ventilation through the walls and ceiling to wick away moisture. But they can also become clogged with minute particles of ice that you won't see. Always make certain you have cross ventilation when cooking inside the tent. Leave the tent flap partially unzipped, and be sure the back vent is open. Do not leave a stove or heater burning when you sleep.

SUN AND SKIERS

The winter sun may not warm your chilled bones, but it might play havoc with your eyes. Few things are more painful than even a mild case of snow-blindness.

You can burn your beak as fast in Arctic conditions as you can in the tropics, so protect what little skin will be exposed to the sun. Use both a blocking agent, to keep the sun's potent ultraviolet rays from reaching your skin, and a moisturizing oil, to keep your skin from cracking.

Sunscreen manufacturers have recently begun using Sun Protection Factor (SPF) numbers on the packaging that indicate the protective strength; the higher the number, the more protection the product offers. For example, SPF 4 means the protection against sunburn is increased four times, and you can stay out in the sun four times longer than you could using no protection at all.

Since lips are particularly vulnerable to wind and sun, always keep a lip salve or sun screen in your pocket, too.

SUNGLASSES

You should never go out without your sunglasses, no matter how overcast the weather. You can suffer from snowblindness even on a cloudy day, because the light that gets through the clouds reflects off the snow.

The most popular ski glasses seem to be the mirrored lenses, which reflect both heat and light and can filter out up to 90 percent of the ultraviolet rays.

Polarized lenses, some of which are also mirrored, are treated to eliminate glare from horizontal surfaces, such as snow, ice, water, and metal.

Photochromatic lenses react to the sun by growing darker as the light brightens and lighter as it fades. These lenses, which are also popular in normal glasses, must be "seasoned" through wear before the change works properly.

When buying sunglasses, keep these factors in mind:

■ They should fit properly and snugly; use elastic bands that are attached to the frames and around your head to keep from losing them.

■ Lenses should be impact-resistant to avoid injuries.

■ Lenses should be optically correct, because distortions can create mo-

guls or other obstacles where none exist.

For contact-lens wearers, keep in mind that glass breaks more easily than plastic, but plastic scratches more easily. The advantage of plastic is that it cuts down on fog, which is a major problem for skiers who wear glasses or contacts.

Glasses that have metal frames which curl around the ears are less likely to fall off than other types. But you should go to an optician for plastic tubes to cover these frames and keep the frigid metal off your skin. Some skiers coat metal frames with lacquer.

Fogging is by far the worst problem with glasses and contacts; here are a few methods of controlling it:

■ Anti-fog cloths and solutions may work sometimes, but glycerin will last longer than the solutions.

■ A chamois cloth will take off moisture faster than anything else while you're on the trail.

■ Put some soap on the inside of the lenses, rub it in, and wipe them dry. This will help considerably.

Double-lens goggles are a big help, because they equalize the temperatures between your face and the outside air.

One of the most elaborate fog-preventive systems is a type of goggle with battery-operated fans that shoot bursts of air inside to clear the glass.

Most experienced x-c skiers agree that contacts are by far the best solution. Glasses and goggles are designed to be worn at least an inch from the eyes, which changes your perception. However, contacts are designed to virtually be a part of your eyes.

CHAPTER 10

EMERGENCIES

EMERGENCY EVACUATION

Sometimes an injured or sick winter camper will still be mobile but unable to ski, due to a stomach ailment, a sprained or broken arm, or a dislocated shoulder. If the victim is able to walk without sustaining further injury, you or a companion can break trail ahead of him and, if necessary, go back and help him walk along the trail.

You can also load the victim on back of your skis, if he is able, making a long downhill run using a very slow, controlled snowplow all the way down to make it a safe ride.

When the victim cannot move under his own power, you have no choice but to carry or drag him out. Since you will be on snow, carrying him is a risky venture at best, unless you are on flat ground and have snowshoes and an adequate litter.

So the best method is to build a sled using the victim's skis. Unfortunately, even the best sled creates a laborious evacuation, and makeshift ones made of skis are even worse. But if that is all you have, you must be able to use it.

Lash the skis together, about shoulder-width apart, by using the ski poles as the cross members, forming an "X." The sled will have to be reinforced with snowshoes, branches and bows, or pack frames, depending on what is available.

When you get under way, put one

person in front to pull the sled and another behind with a rope to help keep the sled off the front person's skis when going downhill and then to help push when going uphill. On extremely steep slopes, you may have to climb to the top with a long rope and then belay the victim up. Unfortunately, the victim will be jostled and bumped along in discomfort, but this is not an easy task under any circumstances.

In extreme emergencies you may not be able to build even a crude sled. Then you have no choice but to put the victim in a sleeping bag or two, wrap him in tarps, ponchos, or tent flies, and simply drag him across the snow, like a stuntman behind a stagecoach in a western.

This is obviously the worst possible situation, and unless you're out in the furthest reaches of the wilderness, such as in Northern Canada or Alaska, this will never happen. In nearly every case, rescue by helicopter or professionals such as ski patrols will only be a matter of a few hours.

AVALANCHES

Few natural dangers are more feared than avalanches, and few have been studied more in recent years. Avalanches are an intimate part of European history, particularly in the Swiss and French Alps, where the direction of wars has turned almost instantly because of avalanches wiping out invading armies.

In North America, avalanches are limited almost entirely to the Rocky Mountains and the lower ranges to the west, the Sierra Nevadas and the Cascades. Avalanches have occurred in the mountains of New England but not

with the regularity and intensity seen in the western mountains.

Explaining and predicting avalanches is not simply mathematical yet, although research is making headway. So many of the factors that create avalanches are hidden beneath the snow's surface that predictions are still largely guesswork. Thus, winter travelers must assume the worst of conditions when they traverse the slopes.

Rather than attempt a detailed description of what happens to snow when it reaches the ground and creates avalanche conditions, we will concentrate on what the average layman should know about avalanches: how to avoid them, how to survive them, and how to rescue people caught in them.

Reduced to its most basic explanation, an avalanche occurs when a given amount of snow becomes too heavy for whatever is holding it in place. It then breaks loose and slides downhill. There are many variables in this over-simplified explanation, but this is essentially what happens.

Avalanches are divided into two general categories: loose snow and slab.

A loose-snow avalanche usually starts at a single point, such as a skier's track, and spreads out like a fan or a pyramid in a chain reaction. One crystal breaks another free, which multiplies as the loose snow moves downhill. Sometimes these avalanches stop after only a few feet, but sometimes they move thousands of tons of snow downhill in speeds of up to 300 miles per hour, creating a shock wave that can flatten parts of a forest that are not even touched by the actual avalanche. An avalanche can roar down a mountainside, creating

Loose Snow Avalanche

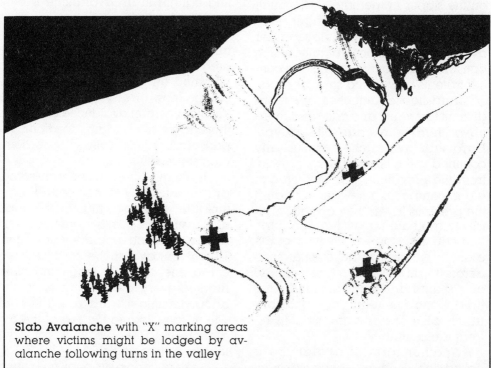

Slab Avalanche with "X" marking areas where victims might be lodged by avalanche following turns in the valley

a storm of flying tiny snow crystals that will rush across the valley and several feet up the other side.

Slab avalanches are those that have a wide area of snow, a plate, that breaks loose in a large piece. This can range in size from just a few square feet to thousands of square feet of snow. The most dangerous and common type of avalanche for skiers is the so-called "soft slab" avalanche. This type occurs most often during or just after a heavy snowfall, when the snow hasn't yet had a chance to settle and adhere to the existing snow. The heavier and the wetter the snow and the colder the temperature, the less likely the new snow will form a bond with the existing snow.

After a heavy snowfall, it is best to treat all snow as having a potential avalanche factor. Those who go out on the slopes immediately after such a snowfall are scouting danger.

The most dangerous place under avalanche conditions is a gully, which can funnel a slab avalanche and concentrate its power in a smaller area.

Hard-slab avalanches are more difficult to predict and can raise more havoc than the average soft-slab type. Hard-slab avalanches are usually confined to the leeward slopes, away from the prevailing wind, which can aid in compacting new snow against the previous layer; they are also usually formed during low temperatures. You can often detect this type of avalanche when you ski or snowshoe across it; you will hear a hollow sound or a slight rumbling, which indicates that the snow beneath you is unstable. In this case, a hasty and smooth retreat is essential.

Another form of avalanche is called the "climax," because it involves several layers of snow instead of only the surface. This type is virtually impossible to sense or predict; fortunately, it occurs quite rarely.

AVOIDING AVALANCHES

The best way to avoid an avalanche is to stay away from slopes of more than twenty-five degrees, which are naturally susceptible to danger. If you stay on broad plains, well away from slopes, avalanches will always happen to other people in other ski areas.

However, most skiers in mountainous areas are not willing to miss the experience of the rugged backcountry when they feel the chance of getting caught in an avalanche is only minor.

The basic ways to avoid an avalanche is to know the history of the area in which you are skiing. Also keep informed on weather conditions, because most areas prone to avalanches interpret avalanche conditions through regular, daily weather reports. In the field, follow these common-sense rules.

If you must cross a dangerous area, try to cross it above the so-called "fracture line," staying as high on the slope as possible. If this is impossible, ski across the slope, one skier at a time. Tie on your avalanche cord, which is a red line, fifty feet long, and often marked every few feet or meters with a tag pointing toward you. The cord will usually float to the top of the avalanche and enable your companions to find you quickly.

Take your pole straps off your wrists

so that if you are caught in an avalanche, you can quickly rid yourself of your poles, which may injure you. You'll also need your hands to cover your face so you can have a small breathing space and possibly dig yourself out later.

Some skiers loosen their bindings and safety straps so they can get out of their skis, but others do not in case they have a chance to ski out of the avalanche.

Before crossing a dangerous slope, you should zip up all your clothing as snugly as possible to keep snow out of your clothing should you get caught.

If you are caught and can't ski out of the fracture zone, make swimming motions in an attempt to stay on top of the snow. This isn't always possible, obviously, but it can at least keep you closer to the surface.

The best piece of equipment to carry in an avalanche-prone area is an avalanche radio beacon, which is similar to the radios carried by most pilots of small aircraft. This radio is about the size of a cigarette package and should be turned on before crossing dangerous slopes. The beacon will send out a distinctive beep; other members of your party can switch their sets to receive the sound and locate you by establishing a simple search procedure.

Not all avalanches begin with a sudden rush downward. They often begin slowly, which may give you the

Cross potential avalanche areas one at a time. Tie on your avalanche cord.

time to ski out of the way. It is impossible to outrun an avalanche, so if one begins above you, always head for the side, moving at a right angle to the direction of the avalance.

If you are in a big avalanche that prevents you from remaining erect, try to prevent the snow from enclosing you completely—it may compact to become as hard as concrete around you. When you feel yourself slowing up, place both hands near your face and chest, in something like a boxer's stance. Just as you stop, cover your mouth and nose with one hand to keep snow from being forced into your breathing passages. Then try to reach the other arm straight up. This offers you the chance to have one hand showing above the surface but helps only if you know which way is up. Avalanches can be completely disorienting.

Immediately upon stopping, try to make room around your head for breathing before the snow completely hardens. Then begin digging, providing you are certain which direction is upward. It is sometimes possible to get out of the snow without help. If this is impossible, you must force yourself to relax and wait for rescue. If you have breathing space and are warmly dressed, you can survive for days.

RESCUE PROCEDURE

If a companion is trapped in an avalanche, follow these procedures:

Time is vital. Although some avalanche victims have lived for days, the odds are not in their favor. Survival varies from case to case, depending on the victim's ability to create an air space, on his physical condition and mental strength, as well as other factors.

A quick search is essential. If there are only two of you on the outing, the problem is magnified; you must decide immediately between going for help or trying to perform the rescue yourself. You should try for the rescue.

First pinpoint the last place you saw the victim, which gives you a point of reference in case a new snowfall covers the avalanche scars. Then you at least know the victim is downhill from that point.

Make a quick search below this point to see if you can find any trace

---

SKI TIP

Each winter millions and millions of acres of land are covered with snow. Since most of that land does not present an avalanche hazard, thousands and thousands of x-c skiers have never seen an avalanche. (The wise ones don't want to.) You can find out in advance from public land agencies where avalanche dangers exist, and in all fairness to yourself, your companions, and the community as a whole, you should avoid these danger areas at all costs. Rescue work is enormously expensive and time-consuming, and your stubborness about avoiding dangerous areas can result in a rescue effort involving dozens of people and thousands of dollars.

Probe systemati-
cally for victims

of the victim, such as an article of clothing, equipment, or the avalanche cord. Check the terrain for places the victim might be lodged, including trees, boulders, ledges, or curves in the gully.

If this yields no trace of the victim, begin probing. Some ski poles are designed to be screwed or snapped together into a single long pole for this purpose; take the baskets off in either case. If there are several skiers in your party, form a line across the avalanche path and slowly work your way downhill. Push the pole into the snow as deeply as you can; then move forward one step and do it again.

You will know when you strike the victim's body, because it will feel completely different from the snow. You may strike a log or a stump, so before

you start digging, make several probes in the same area. But be careful not to probe so as to cause a puncture wound if you have indeed found the victim.

After you find the victim and dig down to him, treat him for suffocation if he cannot speak or is unconscious. Dig into his mouth and nose to remove all snow; then give mouth-to-mouth resuscitation. Continue until the victim is breathing again. Only after recovery should you remove the victim from the snow, warm him, and evacuate as soon as possible.

While performing an avalanche rescue, you are obviously taking some risk yourself. Other avalanches can occur in the same general area, but it is unlikely that another one will occur immediately in the same path.

In the event that you are with a group of more than four or five, it is wise to send one member back to civilization for help, if it isn't more than an hour's skiing away. A search-and-rescue unit can be dispatched by helicopter or snow machine rapidly enough to save the life of a victim who has breathing space and isn't badly injured. But as a general rule, it is best to concentrate everyone's efforts on the rescue.

SKI TIP

The average adult, relaxed and resting, burns about 1,800 calories a day. That's about 75 calories an hour or 1.25 calories a minute.

The average recreational x-c skier will burn 9 calories a minute. The x-c ski racer will burn up to 35 calories a minute.

You can use this information as a guide to comfort on the trail. As you ski, your muscles burn calories to produce heat that keeps you warm. The more motion—the more vigorously you ski—the more calories burned and the less clothing is required.

This emphasizes the importance of layering, which lets you peel off outer garments as needed to maintain a comfortable balance.

EMERGENCY GEAR

It is important that your car contain certain emergency items the year-round, as well as additional tools for winter travel. Some items are obvious, such as a spare tire, jack, and lug wrench. Some people assume that they'll never need these items and remove them to make room for their skiing gear. In a word, don't.

Your car should contain the following:

- Spare tire, jack, and tire tools
- Tire chains that fit—know how to install them
- Heavy rope or tow cable, not only for yourself but for other travelers, as well
- Flares
- Short-handled shovel
- Axe, hatchet, or folding pruning saw
- File
- Assorted nuts, bolts, springs, etc.
- Needles and thread
- Spare fan belt(s)
- Plastic tarp
- Metal water bucket
- Multiple screwdriver set
- Crescent wrench
- Pliers, slip-joint (water pump), and vice grips
- Electrical tape
- Six-foot length, coiled, soft steel wire
- Battery jumper cable
- Duct tape

In addition to these well-established rules of conduct, here are a few more good manners that should be mentioned:

- Heed trail signs. If you find a sign telling you that you're going in the wrong direction, turn around. If a trail is marked closed, don't use it. It is probably closed for a good reason, such as your own safety.
- Don't take pets on trails, for a number of reasons: they make messes on the snow; they can trip other skiers; and they may become exhausted in deep snow. If you want to take your pet along with you, find a place where there are no other skiers.
- If you are going uphill and meet a skier coming down, give him the right-of-way; you have more control than he does.
- Always get permission before going onto private property.
- Don't go for a hike along a ski trail because footprints can ruin a track. If you have a friend or family member who wants to trail along on foot, tell them no.
- When you take a fall and leave a pothole, or "sitzmark," go back and fill it in with snow; if you leave it unfilled, it can be a hazard for other skiers.
- Always pay trail fees where they are posted.

PART IV
EXTENDING YOURSELF: OVERNIGHT EXPEDITIONS

CHAPTER 11

BRAVING THE COLD OUTDOORS

By the time you have progressed this far and have mastered the basics of balance and mobility on your skis, you will want something more adventurous than tramping around the backyard, up and down the street, and around and around the block. You will want to use your skis for what they are intended—to get somewhere on snow without the extra effort and inconvenience found with walking.

The choices are virtually endless, thanks to the relatively low cost of maintaining cross-country ski trails compared with the expense of keeping downhill courses in operation. But mainly, x-c permits you to go wherever you find sufficient snow. You can follow established and maintained tracks and trails, or you can venture off on your own.

The Northeast and Midwest have literally thousands of kilometers of trails marked and maintained for x-c skiing. In Minnesota and Wisconsin alone there are more than 5,500 kilometers of trails, over both flat and rolling country. There are an equal number, if not more, in the northeastern states. The number of kilometers in the western states is probably fewer, but the terrain offers greater challenges, including the mountains and wide open spaces of the high plains and desert.

Many northern state and local park systems have a series of trails especially for x-c skiing; each trail has different characteristics related to length and difficulty. Some have checkpoints where you can stamp your x-c card, much like a self-service passport.

It is virtually impossible to keep a

running total of the thousands of resorts and resort areas across North America that offer maintained and patrolled ski trails. Some are year-round resorts that shift from summer to winter activities; others are primarily winter resorts that close or offer only limited recreation and service during the summer months.

The advantages of planning winter weekends and vacations at these resorts are obvious. They will have qualified instructors available for beginners. Also, repair service and knowledgeable advice on technique and waxing will be included in your package price. Resorts have maintained and well-marked trails, and you will be able to meet other people who are there for the same purpose.

Nearly every national forest headquarters and ranger station in snow country will have information on the best and safest places for skiers, and local ski shops will have either bulletin boards or word-of-mouth information on the best places for ski outings ranging from a few hours to several days.

Downhill ski areas have not ignored the needs of x-c skiing, and more and more of them are finding ways to combine both forms of the sport. For example, in some areas, you can ride a chairlift to the top of the mountain and spend the rest of the day traveling around the peaks and ridges on marked trails, away from the hot-doggers and crowds on the downhill slope.

You are limited only by the terrain and your ingenuity in finding ways to enjoy weekends and vacations with your x-c skis. They can take you almost anywhere you want to go, which is little different than going on day hikes and backpacking trips in the summer. It isn't unusual to see x-c skiers carry-

ing a bag of charcoal and a light-weight grill, or hibachi, as a group decides to go back into the woods a few miles to grill hamburgers or shish-kebab.

CITIZEN RACES

If you are a runner, you are already familiar with citizen races, because the highly publicized marathons, such as those held in Boston and New York, and other lessor known races held throughout North America, are based on the same principle as x-c skiing citizen races. It is obvious that someone will win—and within the horde of participants will be several extremely competitive skiers—but participation is still the main objective.

Perhaps the best known and largest citizens race is at Telemark Lodge near Cable, Wisconsin, which is far up in the northwest corner of the state. The race course is 55 km long and ends in the town of Hayward. It rivals the famous Vasa race in Sweden in number of participants and continues to grow each year. For information on this race, write Telemark Lodge, Cable, WI, 54821.

Many towns and lodges in popular x-c ski areas are organizing similar races. Some of these events are fund-raising drives for charities, but most are simply held for the fun of it.

For information on how to organize a race, write to either the Citizen and Club Cross-Country Racing Committee, U.S. Ski Association, Box 100, Park City, UT, 84060; or the Canadian Ski Association, 333 River Road, Ottawa, Ontario, K1L 8B9.

You can also join one of many outdoor clubs if you want to ski with a group of people who have the same interest. More and more hiking clubs now provide their members with year-round activities by including x-c skiing in their schedule of outings. These clubs often organize groups for low-cost winter trips to Europe, Canada, Alaska, and other regions suitable for skiing vacations. Most clubs find areas that are not overcrowded with downhill skiers, and they have the advantage of visiting foreign countries when the regular tourists are back home. A tourist who arrives in town on a pair of skis rather than in a tour bus will find it much easier to become acquainted.

However you decide to go x-c skiing, you'll find that few other forms of recreation offer you the freedom of travel and the wide choice of places to visit. You'll find numerous places near your home: playfields abandoned to the snow, golf courses closed for the winter, power line rights-of-way, abandoned railroad beds, unpopulated jogging and bike paths, beaches with snow covering the sand, and rolling farmland with an angry bull confined to his winter quarters in the barnyard.

One of the most rewarding ways to enjoy this sport is to go out on a still, cold night when the moon is full and shining on the snow so brightly that you'll remember overcast days that were darker. Some skiers enjoy laying out night courses with lanterns, torches, or even electric lights when available to make the best of the dead of winter.

After you become completely at ease on your skis, one of your first purchases should be a small day pack, if you don't already own one. This will enable you to carry a change of socks and mitten liners, a thermos of hot drinks, a few snack items, your Ten Essentials, and perhaps a stove and cookset.

With this pack you are ready for day-long trips of several kilometers. A log, a high bank beside the road or trail, a broad stump, or a cluster of boulders can serve as your picnic table at lunchtime. You can break up the day's traveling with a brisk game of follow-the-leader, which also helps sharpen your skills, provided the most experienced and swiftest skiers don't make life miserable for the novices. But follow-the-leader is an excellent way to take the trudging aspect out of skiing when you're returning to the car over familiar terrain at the end of a long day.

In many cases, those who start x-c skiing after the first snowfall and get out at least once a week during the winter will by spring be planning tougher trips for the next winter season. These are trips that involve several days' travel in areas where there will likely be no other people. As with any sport, the urge to extend oneself is almost irresistible.

A PRIMER ON SNOW

For most of us, snow is something that is pretty to watch when we're sitting in the dark living room, looking out at the yard with the patio lights on. But it is a bother in the morning, when we have to scrape it off the sidewalk and the driveway before we can leave the garage. It may cause us to be late for work because some nincompoop on the freeway doesn't have his chains

on and causes a traffic jam. It is always the other driver, never ourselves, who causes these things.

Most of us think of snow in very basic, relative terms. We tend to classify it as wet snow, which clings to our ornamental plants but makes excellent snowballs and snowmen, and dry snow, which flies around like down in the slightest breeze and is no good for snowball fights or snowmen. This basic classification system should be the foundation used in deciding which ski wax to use, but only the dedicated skiers think of such things.

Although snow is one of the most complex subjects in nature, it is one of the least-studied parts of our environment. The serious study of snow by the scientific community—the shape of crystals, the composition of various layers of snow, its transformation from individual crystals into water or ice, and hundreds of other aspects—has become popular only in recent years.

For the skier, the characteristics of snow are most important in determining which kind of wax to use. In certain parts of the country, skiers need also to be wary of avalanche dangers, ice, treacherous snow bridges, and the suitability of snow for building shelters, windbreaks, or even igloos.

The International Commission on Snow and Ice has proposed a classification of seven basic forms of falling snow crystals: star, plate, needle, column, column with cap at each end, spatial dentrite, and irregular. But this is only for snow as it falls.

Shortly after this proposal, in 1951, still another classification system was presented that had 101 types of snow crystals, including hollow bullet, solid bullet, hexagonal plate, cup, pyramid, and so on.

Philosophers and scientists have studied snow since the earliest recorded history, but only in recent years have scientists learned how atmospheric conditions create certain shapes of snow flakes, or crystals.

Still, no one, philosopher or scientist, has made a more in-depth study of snow than the people who have lived for centuries around the Arctic Rim—the Lapps, Siberians, and Eskimos. And nobody has better understood the various types of snow nor named the types with one-word definitions. Only a few of these Eskimo and Siberian words have entered the English language. As an example, here are a few words from North American Eskimos and Siberians:

Api - snow not yet picked up by the wind.

Upsik - snow picked up by the wind and deposited in a mass.

Siqoq - snow that is more wind-blown than any other snow.

Vyduv - a place that has been cleared of snow by the wind.

Zaboy - an accumulation of snow blown into a depression and liable to stay there into the summer.

Perhaps as winter recreation becomes more and more popular, some of these terms will gradually work into our language, since they are so succinct. Obviously, the English language has its own terms for snow. Here are a few special forms and types of snow that have been classified by mountaineers and skiers:

Rotten snow is a soft, wet snow, often found in the spring. It is in the lower layers of the snowpack that offer little or no support for weight; sometimes it is so soft, or rotten, that it won't support the weight of a skier on the longest pair of x-c skis. This usually occurs in higher elevations, particularly in the Rockies.

Corn snow usually occurs when the early spring melting process begins and the snow melts slightly; this is then followed by a period of cold weather or cold nights. The melting-freezing process creates small rounded snow crystals that are quite coarse and after the morning thaw give excellent skiing and stepkicking.

Powder snow, that condition sought by so many downhill and x-c skiers, is generally defined as new, light, loose snow. But true powder snow is new snow that has changed its structure somewhat and lost its adhesiveness due to low temperatures. Powder snow can also be dangerous, because it is susceptible to avalanches.

Sun crust is caused by the sun melting the surface of the snow, which then refreezes into a crust of boned snow crystals.

Meltwater crust is almost identical, except that it is caused by warm air or condensation rather than the sun.

Rime is the dense deposit of dull white ice caused by freezing droplets of water on the windward side of objects. Fog is a contributing factor.

Hoarfrost is formed from water vapor in the atmosphere and has crystalline shapes. When it appears on the snow surface as **surface hoar**, it makes for excellent skiing.

Firnspiegel is a thin layer of ice on snow surfaces, usually in spring and summer, and is so brilliant in the sunlight that some call it "glacier fire." When this layer of ice forms, it can act as a greenhouse and permit melting beneath while remaining solid on the surface.

Cornices are one of the most dangerous snow forms for skiers and mountaineers. They form on the leeward side of ridges, hanging over in an unstable mass. They frequently cause or contribute to avalanches. Experienced mountain skiers may learn how to judge their stability, but the wise wilderness skier avoids them.

There are many other snow phe-

Wind Chill Chart

WIND SPEED MPH	COOLING POWER OF WIND EXPRESSED AS "EQUIVALENT CHILL TEMPERATURE"																				
	TEMPERATURE (°F)																				
CALM	40	35	30	25	20	15	10	5	0	-5	-10	-15	-20	-25	-30	-35	-40	-45	-50	-55	-60
	EQUIVALENT CHILL TEMPERATURE																				
5	35	30	25	20	15	10	5	0	-5	-10	-15	-20	-25	-30	-35	-40	-45	-50	-55	-65	-70
10	30	20	15	10	5	0	-10	-15	-20	-25	-35	-40	-45	-50	-60	-65	-70	-75	-80	-90	-95
15	25	15	10	0	-5	-10	-20	-25	-30	-40	-45	-50	-60	-65	-70	-80	-85	-90	-100	-105	-110
20	20	10	5	0	-10	-15	-25	-30	-35	-45	-50	-60	-65	-75	-80	-85	-95	-100	-110	-115	-120
25	15	10	0	-5	-15	-20	-30	-35	-45	-50	-60	-65	-75	-80	-90	-95	-105	-110	-120	-125	-135
30	10	5	0	-10	-20	-25	-30	-40	-50	-55	-65	-70	-80	-85	-95	-100	-110	-115	-125	-130	-140
35	10	5	-5	-10	-20	-30	-35	-40	-50	-60	-65	-75	-80	-90	-100	-105	-115	-120	-130	-135	-145
40	10	0	-5	-15	-20	-30	-35	-45	-55	-60	-70	-75	-85	-95	-100	-110	-115	-125	-130	-140	-150

WINDS ABOVE 40 HAVE LITTLE ADDITIONAL EFFECT.

LITTLE DANGER	INCREASING DANGER (Flesh may freeze within 1 min.)	GREAT DANGER (Flesh may freeze within 30 seconds)

DANGER OF FREEZING EXPOSED FLESH FOR PROPERLY CLOTHED PERSONS

Source: National Weather Service, U.S. Dept. of Commerce

nomena and countless variations in the different regions of North America that come under the heading of local knowledge.

It is always surprising for the novice winter camper to learn that snow is one of nature's best insulators. This is not to say that life inside an igloo is balmy; nevertheless, snow shelters offer a surprisingly cozy place to rest or sleep.

Wheat farmers often speak of the dreaded "open winter" when too little snow falls to cover the young wheat that was planted in the fall. This winter wheat sprouts before winter and grows to about the height of a two-week-old lawn, then goes dormant with cold weather. The usual snowfall then covers the tender shoots and protects them against wind chill and the extreme temperatures. Thus, snow is a blanket that keeps the cold out and traps the natural warmth of the earth.

Ground covered by snow will freeze, of course, but not nearly so easily nor so deeply as bare, open ground. Scientists have found that snow-covered ground will freeze to a depth of one inch, while adjacent bare ground without snow cover will freeze as much as 10 inches to a foot.

Winter travelers can use snow for transportation on the surface, and experienced skiers travel easier on snow than walkers do on bare ground. Ski campers can use snow to build an array of shelves, cooking stands, seats, and tables. They can also use it as a windbreak around their tents to keep considerably more comfortable and warm. They can also use the snow to make complete shelters—snow caves, covered trenches, igloos, and versions of lean-tos.

When understood and used properly, snow is an excellent ally for campers, as well as a silent beauty.

Snow also makes an excellent playground, and few activities are more universal than snow play. Eskimo children, tropical adults seeing snow for the first time, sophisticated urbanites, and senior citizens all respond in the same way to snow. Snowball fights begin almost immediately, and versions of snowmen are soon built. The urge to play with snow is so universal that it has been known to transcend the intellectual boundaries between man and other animals. For example, some species of monkeys have been observed amusing themselves by making a snowball and rolling it along to make it grow to such dimensions that they can no longer push it. When snow falls, people are included among the mammals who almost involuntarily lean back their heads and stick out their tongues to catch the snowflakes.

Snow is a great natural reservoir, not only for water for summer use after the slow melting of the snowpack, but also as a slow release mechanism for nutrients present in water when it evaporates and is reintroduced to the cycle of precipitation. Sulphate, calcium, potassium, nitrates, and other soil nutrients are stored in snow and can be of more value to soil than rainfall, which may run off before it has an opportunity to penetrate the soil.

Even though snow is fun and functional, it is obviously not without its dangers. These include cave-ins, avalanches, and the common health hazards of cold weather such as frostbite, freezing, and, strangely enough, dehydration. Snow represents an extreme in climate that can be dangerous, just like summer or tropical sun. But rather than fear snow and winter, it is best to become knowledgeable and learn to live within the limitations it offers.

AWAY FROM THE BEATEN TRACKS

Once you've found familiarity and comfort on x-c skis, you will feel the urge to continue your trips to car campgrounds and on into the backcountry. There is no reason not to do so, because snow travel and camping offers you experiences quite different from traveling and camping in the same areas during the warm-weather months.

After you have mastered the skis, the next major consideration is to learn how to deal with the cold and the absence of heat, as well as how to make certain that the heat produced naturally by your body is protected by your clothing and sleeping gear.

You must keep the cold out and the heat in. It is that simple. But maintaining the balance between your body and the environment is an incredibly complex situation. We often complicate it for ourselves by worrying more about appearance than function in our clothing. We endanger ourselves by our general lack of experience in the outdoors and by not following the proper advice that has been available ever since man settled along the Arctic latitudes.

Since most of us gain our knowledge of wilderness situations from books, we frequently forget that some texts are written for specific situations rather than for the worst or the mildest situations. An example of this confusion is the matter of sleeping in the cold.

Perhaps millions of people associate sleeping in the cold with death, the last stage of hypothermia. Yet Eskimos and other experienced Arctic travelers have always considered sleep as a pleasant way to pass the time while lost and the best way to save your energy and keep calm. So, when we read Vilhjalmur Stefansson's four rules for surviving a blizzard in the Arctic, we are confused:

- Keep still and move only to stay warm.
- Don't overexert and sweat because it dampens clothing.
- Build a shelter of some sort, preferably of snow if the temperature drops to -10° F.
- Sleep as much as possible.

It is the fourth rule that confuses some people, because they probably have never been in that situation and actually fear sleep. Yet, they have had the experience of waking up on a cold night with the covers off and knowing it was the cold that caused them to wake. This is exactly what Stefansson and the Eskimos with whom he lived knew: When a blizzard strikes and you become totally disoriented, if you are dressed properly, sleep is one of the four requisites for staying alive. When you become chilled, the cold will wake you; so you will get up, walk around a bit or exercise to restore circulation and natural body heat, and then sit back down again.

Stefansson grew up on a North Dakota farm and learned the basics of winter survival there by making a few mistakes that frightened him enough to make him want to learn. Then while he was living with the Eskimos, he learned more. One of his favorite stories was about the elderly Eskimo woman who was caught by a blizzard no more than half an hour from home. She knew better than to try to find home in the blizzard, so she simply sat to wait out the storm. She sat in the same place three days and nights, getting up occasionally to exercise. But she knew she could live long enough to wait out the storm without the fear of starving to death.

No matter where you live and where you go for your outdoor recreation, you face dangers from nature. You must dress properly for the desert, just as you must dress properly for the snow. You shouldn't camp in dry washes in the desert because of the flash flood danger, and you shouldn't camp in avalanche paths in the mountains or on frozen lakes unless you know the depth and condition of both the ice and snow beneath you. Just because the snow is deep does not mean the ice is thick enough for safety; a thawing period which turned the ice into slush could have been followed by a heavy wet snowfall.

Before you try winter travel and camping, you should know something about your own body. Do you get cold easier than most people, or are you one of those who suffer during the summer heat and look forward to winter so you won't feel sweaty all the time? Do you have good circulation, or are your extremities susceptible to sudden changes in temperature? When you ask yourself these questions, be honest. It is no time for bluffing.

Each of us has a slightly different physiological makeup than our contemporaries, subtle differences that must be taken into consideration for all activities, indoor and out, winter and summer. Since most of the population lives in the temperate zones, our bodies are more accustomed to moderate changes in our environment rather than the dramatic changes of the polar area.

Few of us have developed the characteristics that aid survival for the Eskimos and Indians around the tip of South America. Those people have made adjustments over the centuries that allow them more comfort in extremes. Their hands stay warmer than ours because more than half again as much blood flows into their fingers. Their bodies maintain a higher core temperature and recover from chilling faster. The Alacaluf Indians of Tierra del Fuego have similar characteristics. It isn't uncommon to see them swimming in the ocean while sleet is in the air. They go barefooted much of the time, partly by choice and partly because they have few materials from which to make shoes.

Obviously, few of us can bear as much cold. We must dress properly, eat foods that produce both energy and body heat, and take no chances.

However, dwelling on the potential problems caused by cold weather isn't doing justice to x-c skiing and related activities. The incidence of injury and death among winter recreationists is low, in part because most people who go out in the winter are usually prepared for emergencies, sometimes more so than when they go out in the summer. Most x-c skiers and snow travelers are careful to select good weather for their trips and to take fewer chances than normal.

The Boy Scout motto of always being prepared is never more important than in the winter, because proper preparation is what gives you the freedom to move anywhere you want to go without having to worry that you may be out of your element and in danger. A major factor in being prepared is to have the proper equipment for extended winter treks.

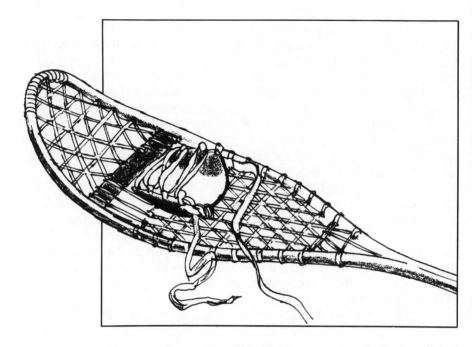

(top) Maine/ Michigan snow shoe (bottom) Metal claws for traction

SNOWSHOES

Only a few years ago, before x-c skiing took over as the major form of winter transportation and recreation, snowshoeing was "discovered" by Americans. Books were written and manufacturers went to double shifts to keep up with the demand. Now

snowshoeing has slipped back to its original position and will probably remain there, thanks to the versatility of x-c skis, which is now taken for granted.

Compared with x-c skiing, snowshoeing seems pedestrian if not a bit awkward. But there are still many, many people who get around on snowshoes during the winter, so they'll always have their place in winter transportation systems. They are more utilitarian than skis, which makes them favored by workmen, farmers, ranchers, trappers, fishermen, and hunters. How, for example, would you pack out an elk while on x-c skis? With snowshoes, it is simple.

If you are going winter camping, you will need a pair of snowshoes from time to time, and many winter campers consider them as much a part of their equipment at cooking utensils. They weigh little, can easily be strapped on the back of a pack, and are almost indispensable around the camp when you're on loose snow. Given the choice of walking down to the stream for water wearing snowshoes or boots, anyone would choose snowshoes over post-holing down and back.

In fact, at times you'll probably prefer snowshoes to skis, because your plans may call for packing equipment into a particular basin or wildlife area and staying within sight of camp the whole time while you take photographs or simply enjoy the winter landscape. In this case, skis might even be a bother.

Using snowshoes is so simple that no instructions or detailed charts and graphs are needed. They are awkward at first, and the most common mistake you'll make will be to take spraddle-legged strides until you learn how far to spread your legs without whacking your calves and ankles. On your first outing or two, your leg muscles will get a bit stiff but will become accustomed to snowshoes, just as you will become comfortable with them.

Remember to watch how wide your stride is, and learn to spread your legs only as much as needed. Avoid excessive lifting; the tail of the snowshoe is supposed to be dragged, so when you lift your foot, don't try to lift the whole thing out of the snow. If you do, you'll look and feel like a cow walking in a bog, and you'll also expend energy unnecessarily.

If you're climbing steep slopes, you may have to attach crampons to your boots to get traction. Avoid using snowshoes as bridges across depressions, because the edges alone aren't designed to support your weight; the frame and lacing provide the support together.Some winter resort areas like to sponsor snowshoe events such as softball games. But you'll soon find that snowshoes aren't the mode of transportation for those who are in a hurry. True, you can run in them, but if you're intent on covering a lot of miles on a trip, you should be on skis. The best pace for snowshoes is a leisurely one, which encourages you to take more careful note of your surroundings. And since you're much less likely to fall on snowshoes than on skis, you can compare snowshoeing with an old-fashioned Sunday afternoon drive, where you look at the fence posts and mailboxes instead of the center line of the speedway.

MAJOR TYPES OF SNOWSHOES

Although there are several variations, three major snowshoe designs remain popular:

Maine and Michigan: These are the largest and widest, usually 12 to 14 inches across, and have the longest tail. They are best in open timber or meadows, rather than brush, because their length and width cause them to become entangled in brambles and underbrush. They come in a wide variety of sizes to support everyone from adults to children.

Alaska or Pickerel: This is a long and narrow design, which is usually only 10 inches wide and up to 60 inches long. It is the fastest design and well-suited to packed snow and open country.

Bear Paw: There are several variations of this rather round and short design, which are by far the best for traveling in brushy country where you have to twist and turn and backtrack. Because they are so wide, they are also best for carrying heavy loads, such as a big person and heavy pack. This type is usually 14 inches wide and between 33 and 36 inches long. Some varieties are oblong and others more oval. The type you chose should depend on the kind of snow you'll be traveling on, the kind of load you'll be carrying, and your own weight. One variation called the "Sherpa" is favored by mountaineers because it is lighter, has metal claws built into the pivoting harness, and has a sheet of nylon neoprene instead of traditional lacing.

MATERIALS

The snowshoe frame is made of either aluminum or white ash; each material has its own advantages. Aluminum is obviously the lightest, so more and more snowshoes are being built of that framework.

The lacing is either cowhide or a synthetic, such as neoprene. Synthetics are becoming more popular, be-

cause cowhide stretches when wet. Also, rodents aren't attracted to the lacings when they're made of a synthetic material.

PULKAS/SLEDS

Although most skiers headed for the backcountry on a three-day or longer trip carry their camping equipment on their backs, it is worth noting that the experts on winter travel—Lapps and Eskimos—preferred not to. If they didn't use sled dogs or reindeer, they towed their gear along behind them in sleds that one person could easily handle. This was due in part to the common terrain of land above the Arctic Circle, which is free of dense timber and jagged mountain ranges.

But one suspects that even if the terrain hadn't been flattened over the centuries by glaciers, the Lapps and Eskimos would still opt for another method of transporting heavy loads. Carrying weight on your back across the snow is not only very tiring, it is also awkward.

Thus, the **pulka**, a Lapp word for a toboggan, was used for centuries before mechanized vehicles arrived. Old woodcuts show pulkas being towed by reindeer as well as men. They were a standard form of winter transportation.

Pulkas are making a comeback of sorts for both convenience and safety factors. Backpacks restrict your movement; if you fall, it is difficult to get back up again. And should you break through ice with a pack on, your problems multiply.

Granted, toboggans are more useful on very long expeditions, where

Pulka

food for several days or even weeks is needed. But they are a reasonable alternative to carrying a 60-pound pack that restricts your mobility and tires you as you make your way through the snow.

The classic Alaskan and Canadian sled with runners that protrude from the bottom is of limited use for most recreational skiers, because it bites into the snow. Such a sled is useful only in the Arctic where there is firmly packed snow; then the runners can be dampened to build a film of ice on the runner bottoms.

Thus, the sleds used in most parts of the United States and lower Canada are actually toboggans, sometimes modified with shallow runners that serve only as guides.

The best sleds are designed so that they can only be loaded and unloaded from one side, which prevents having to hop around to both sides to unsnap the cover. These sleds also have a grommet-and-snap system so you can open and close the cover without having to remove your mittens.

Another feature to look for in a pulka is that the sides slope outward, which will allow the sled to right itself. Also remember that shallow runners are usually needed to keep the pulka tracking, but such runners are not for support, as they are on Arctic dog sleds.

The harness for pulling a sled consists of a belt that is connected to a towing line. Some come with a spring-loaded shock absorber that smooths out the inevitable jerking that will occur on up-and-down terrain. Although most have very slick bottoms, they can be waxed for even better performance. These sleds pull so easily that, even when fully loaded, they drag only when being pulled uphill. On level ground they require virtually no additional effort. And they are designed so that they are difficult to overturn and will not slide sideways.

Many toboggan and sled devotees pack everything except a very light load that they carry in their knapsack, such as a lunch, ski repair kit, wax kit, and other small and lightweight items.

One winter camping expert, Bob Gary, tells in his book **Winter Camping** (Stephen Greene Press, 1979) how he and his companions divide the labor into two roles: the "mule," who tows the sled, and the "trailbreaker," who goes ahead of the mule to prepare the route. When climbing a hill, the trailbreaker goes back behind to help the mule and give the sled a push with his ski pole or hands. If the hill is extremely steep, they may choose to attach a long length of climbing rope to the sled and climb the hill before starting to muscle the sled up. Going downhill, the trailbreaker falls behind to hold the sled off the mule by using a rope attached to the rear.

Sled devices aren't for everyone and are certainly not suitable for mountainous areas or terrain marked with boulders and stumps. Then a sled may be more trouble than struggling along with the load on your back.

As more skiers head for the wilderness on extended trips, the use of pulkas will grow. And once you have a pulka, you will find a variety of uses for it, not only on ski trips but at home, as well. For example, pulkas are commonly used as baby carriages. Just make sure that the sled has a headrest and some kind of roll-bar arrangement. Frequently the windshield and headrest serve as this safety feature.

A pulka is also handy for towing home the groceries when you decide to leave the car in the garage, for transporting food and equipment to the cabin beyond the end of the road.

SNOW SHELTERS

Snow caves and igloos have become very popular among winter campers. Just how many campers actually use and rely on them is unknown, but these natural shelters have many supporters in the outdoor fraternity. In fact, on-the-site construction is always part of winter survival training.

Whether you ever actually use one of these shelters, you should learn how to build one by actually doing so. If nothing else, you will have the security of knowing you can build one if necessary. Besides, they're fun to build and crawl into.

The most common shelter is the snow cave, because it's the easiest to build. To do so, you must first find the proper type of snow; a vertical wall of wind-blown snow that has formed a deep drift is the best, since windblown snow will be packed tighter than ordinary snow.

You will need two diggers, one to go in first and shovel out the snow, and the other to remove the snow from the tunnel as it progresses. The best shovel to carry is one with a short "D" handle and a steel blade. The aluminum snow shovels carried by many snow campers are not sturdy enough for heavy work.

The entrance tunnel should be only slightly larger than your body, so you must crawl into it. After digging a few feet in, you can gradually expand the tunnel until you have a large dome-shaped room. Unless you are in an extremely large drift, you won't be able to stand erect in the completed room, but you can make it large enough so two or three people can camp in comfort.

The important aspect is to keep the

Building a
snow cave

wall-roof very smooth, having no serrated surfaces from the shovel, because these edges invariably create drips when the heat from your body, stoves, and lights warms the interior. The interior wall-ceiling will soon develop a glaze of ice that acts as further support for the cave.

When the cave is complete, you should punch a hole through the ceiling for ventilation. Some campers carry long aluminum tubes that are made of interconnecting pieces to serve both as ventilation pipes and flag poles that mark the cave when you go out for the day.

Once the basic work is done, you can emulate the Eskimos and build sleeping platforms where you can stretch out your pad and sleeping bag and lie in comfort. Then if you're committed to architecture, you can also build small snow shelves for your cooking utensils. You will do most of your cooking from a prone position, so the stove and utensils should be within reach of the cave dwellers.

A snow cave can be used for several days as a base camp, but you should be certain it is marked well, either by a long pole or some other such marker. It is both embarrassing and dangerous to come back from a day's skiing and not be able to find your home after snow has either blown over the opening or so much new snow has fallen that every drift looks alike. Then, your best hope is that you can find your cave with a probe of some kind, or that you will fall through the roof. You'll have to build another cave, but at least you'll have your equipment.

For protection against drifts during the night, you can build blocks of snow to create a baffle system of doors at the entrance, or you can hang a piece of tarp or some other material over the entrance, making certain the ventilation holes on top are free.

Igloos are another matter and not nearly so easy to build. But they are necessary in open meadows or other areas where no drifts occur. They are a lot more work but once built will last longer than a cave and provide a more sturdy shelter.

You may have to stamp out a large

TRENCH SHELTER

Build A Trench Shelter to Wait Out The Storm

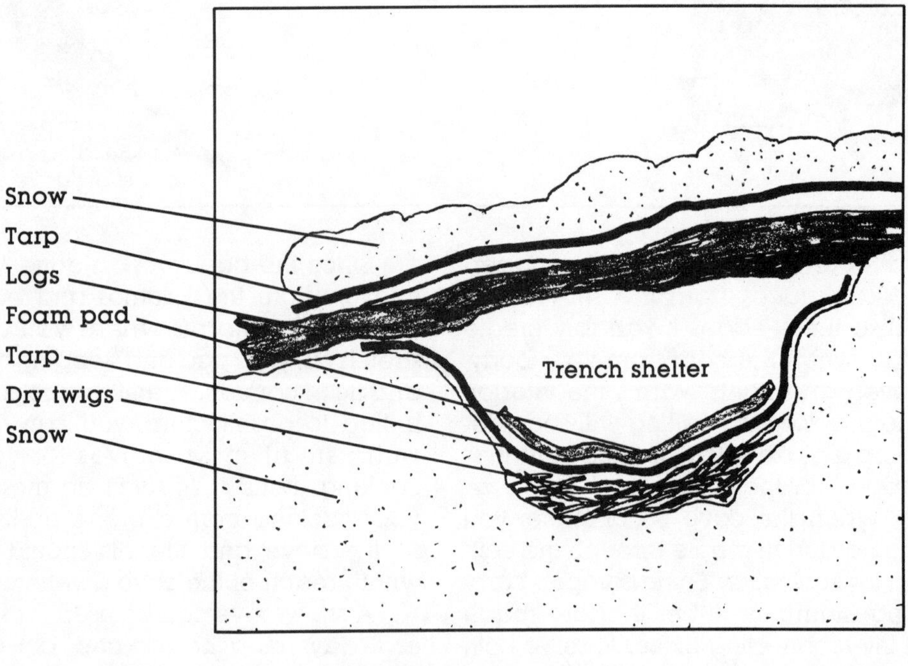

Snow —
Tarp —
Logs —
Foam pad —
Tarp —
Dry twigs —
Snow —

Trench shelter

square of snow to be sure it is firm enough to be cut into blocks and carried to your construction site. As with building the cave, it is best to work with two persons. One will cut and carry the snow blocks, and the other will stand inside the circle of blocks and slowly build them upward and inward, providing chinking on both the inside and outside to keep the walls wind- and snowproof.

Igloos shouldn't be built any larger than necessary, because they are a lot of work to build and the smaller ones have the most structural strength. They can be enlarged by digging down through the snow and shoveling the unwanted snow out the door.

The door can be as simple or complex as you want it. Depending on the weather, you may want a simple opening in one wall that you can cover with a pack or snow block. Or you can build a long entry tunnel with a curve in it to act as a baffle for the wind.

As with caves, you can build sleeping shelves and a variety of other snow furniture inside an iglo. Some campers who have a lot of nervous energy to burn build elaborate igloos, even split levels, or build several to create an igloo village with connecting passageways.

The most basic snow shelters are covered trenches or bivouacs. These are usually emergency shelters only and not designed for extended occupancy. If you are caught out in a storm or have misjudged the length of your day's trip and darkness is falling, a trench or bivouac may easily save your life.

To make a trench shelter, take off your skis and use them as shovels for digging a trench. Line the bottom of the trench with evergreen boughs, or

preferably your sleeping pad, if you're carrying it. Use whatever you can to keep your body off the snow. Then cover the trench with snow blocks, if you can carve them out, and stack them over you like a long tent.

If you can't use snow blocks, your next choice is your skis and poles or snowshoes. Find more branches to give cover and pack them with snow so that you are beneath a crude cover.

If you have the time and the digging tools, you can build a substantial trench bivouac, which is closed at the foot and protected from drifts at the head. But you usually don't have time to be choosy about your shelter; if you did, you would build a cave or igloo.

EDDIE BAUER
EXPEDITIONS

Most cross-country skiers can tolerate equipment that isn't "just right," even for the few hours that most outings last. Perhaps your ski's camber isn't just right or the length is off a few millimeters. Or maybe your layering system of clothing doesn't seem quite versatile enough for those awkward temperatures when it is too warm to wear a sweater, yet too cold to go without. Things may never be absolutely perfect, but if you plan your equipment purchases properly and make your outing a brief one, you should be able to go out and enjoy yourself without being in danger.

But if you are on an expedition hundreds or thousands of miles away from the nearest condominium or trail head, you must be prepared for the worst possible conditions. This is especially true when going on an expedition to the far corners of the Arctic in the dead of winter.

As part of its research into proper clothing for the worst conditions this planet can offer, Ed-

die Bauer, Inc., has participated in the sponsorship of numerous mountaineering and Arctic overland expeditions. A partial list includes:

1953—The American K2 Himalayan Expedition
1955—The International Himalayan Expedition
1958—The American Himalayan Expedition to Gasherbrum
1963—The American Everest Expedition
1973—Dhaulagiri Himalayan Expedition
1978—Baffin Island Expedition
1979—Vatnajokull Glacier, Iceland

1980—John Roskelley's attempt on Makalu
1980—First woman's attempt on Dhaulagiri
1981—Svalbard Expedition, Norway
1982—Ellesmere Island Crossing
1983—the West. Ridge Mt. Everest Expedition

Each of these expeditions test garments and sleeping equipment under extreme circumstances. On three expeditions—Baffin Island, Svalbard, and Ellesmere Island treks—the use of cross-country skis and sleds was essential.

Alan Errington, co-leader of the expeditions, said that on one of its earlier trips the group attempted to use waxable skis but found that they were difficult because of the extremes in temperatures and snow conditions. The group would travel in warm valleys with soft snow on one day and in higher elevations with temperature extremes the next. Consequently, the group felt it was spending half of the day waxing skis.

After that experience, the expeditions were outfitted with waxless skis, which Errington found to be so practical and durable that they didn't really need

to carry spares. The group used wrapped box core models that were so tough that "we have bent some almost double with no damage."

In addition to the skis, clothing, and sleeping bags, the group had to be quite conscious of maintaining proper nutrition for the extremes in temperature. When the temperature was only −25° F, each person consumed 4,000 calories per day. But when the temperature fell to −40° F and the windchill factor hit −125° F or lower, the caloric intake was increased to 25,000 per person. The group ate lots of cheese, butter, and sausage because of their high fat content.

The group took one sled per person. These were actually small toboggans since they had no runners. Sleds with runners didn't work well because of varying snow conditions.

Each sled was loaded with 200 pounds of food and equipment at the start of the trip. As the trip progressed, the skiers had no difficulty in covering 25 miles a day while carrying 100 pounds in their sleds. The only problem they experienced with the sleds was that they had a tendency to tip on steep slopes. Going downhill was simple—they just hung on to the ropes and let the sled go under its own weight!

CHAPTER 12

CAMPING EQUIPMENT

With a few obvious differences, the camping equipment you use on summer backpacking trips can be used for winter camping. Thus, the following information is based on the ultralight, compact backpacking equipment now available.

PACKS

The standard pack for most activities is the external-frame design, which comes in two separate parts: the frame and the pack that attaches to it. This is the best design for carrying heavy loads because it keeps the load away from your back; the weight is borne on your hips and to a much lesser extent your shoulders.

External-frame pack: One advantage of the frame pack is that it offers two and sometimes three compartments with pockets on the sides, another smaller compartment that can be attached below for additional gear or your sleeping bag, and still another detachable sack that fits on top of the main sack.

Most backpackers are content with having the main compartment for clothing, food, cooking equipment, and tools. Then they strap their tent above the sack and their sleeping bag on the bottom. You have several choices in this matter, and it makes no great difference which style you choose.

The major disadvantage of external-frame packs for snow camping and cross-country touring is that they are a bit unwieldy for backcountry trips

on skis or snowshoes; they can get in the way of your poling and stick up so far that they easily snag on bushes. Packs can also be very awkward in the inevitable falls skiers take. Some of these problems can be avoided if your pack has a removable top section. In this case, you can take the top bar off and strap your tent or sleeping bag to the pack itself.

Internal-frame pack: This is the most popular design with x-c skiers, because the best ones fit snugly against your back and bend and twist with you rather than hang rigidly from a frame. The framework is built into the sack, and many are adjustable so that they conform to different heights and needs. Like the external-frame packs, they have a padded hipbelt that supports most of the load and shoulder straps to help with the weight and keep the pack snugly against your back.

Soft packs: This design has no frame at all and is best known as a rucksack or knapsack. Their load capacity is considerably less than that of the other two designs, which is best for shorter trips or for day use when you want to take along a lunch, a stove, and extra clothing.

TIPS ON BUYING A PACK

It is important to try packs on with weight in them. All packs feel great when you swing them onto your shoulders in the store. But after they're packed with 50 or 60 pounds, they feel entirely different. When you get one on your back in the store with the approximate load you will be carrying, don't be shy about going through all the body motions you will experience on the trail. Bend over, lean sideways, walk around, climb stairs, and go through the poling and striding mo-

tions. Keep fiddling with the belt and shoulder straps to be sure you can adjust them properly.

Check out different kinds of packs by renting them for weekend outings. Not every brand of pack is right for everyone, so try packs by different manufacturers. When you buy a pack, you are making an investment that might last the rest of your outdoor life; packs seldom have to be discarded because they wear out.

Packs come in front-load and top-load designs; decide which type you prefer. The top-load models require

you to stuff everything in from the top. Some people prefer this because they're not especially concerned with being neat and tidy; they know that most people are careful packers only when they are packing at home. When out on the trail, with cold hands and other things to do, they simply cram things in and get going.

Front-load designs usually open the whole back of the pack so that everything is in plain view. These are perhaps the best for in-camp use because you can lay the pack flat and have everything easily available. But on the

trail, you may have difficulty keeping things in the pack when it is zipped open by a mate in search of a pair of socks or a first-aid kit. Another potential problem is the danger of having a zipper snag, freeze, or tear out entirely during a trip.

Hip belts: Be sure your pack has the best padded hip belt available and that it is your size. It is essential that it have a quick-release buckle, in case you fall through the ice or a snow bridge into a stream or in case you "turn turtle" and must crawl out of the pack that is holding you flat on your back in the snow. The buckle is also important for another reason: You should be able to tighten or loosen the belt without having to take off your gloves or mittens. Spring-loaded clamps that grip the webbed belt are the simplest and safest to use.

Pockets: It is a good idea to have at least three side pockets, one that runs the full length of the pack and two that are shorter. You can put longer items, such as tall fuel bottles, collapsible saws, or spare ski tips, in the longest pocket and smaller items, such as toilet gear, first-aid kit, stove spare parts, and candles, in the smaller ones.

Accessories: It's impossible to have too many straps on the outside of the pack. You'll need someplace to hang your ice axe, skis, snowshoes, climbing rope, and other gear that you will want to reach quickly. Many packs have leather slots sewn on the top or bottom for strapping sleeping bags or tents; again, you can never have too many.

Materials: New fabrics are continually introduced on the market. Most of them are some form of nylon with names such as Cordura, and all but the least expensive fabrics are extremely rugged. Tearing isn't a com-

PACKS

From bottom to top: belt or fanny pack, rucksack, external frame pack.

Ski mountaineering pack

mon problem but split seams and faulty stitching can be. Check the stitching first; make sure it is even, between 5 and 10 stitches per inch. The seams are where most leaks occur in waterproof packs, so you need either a stick of seam sealer or a waterproof pack cover; a cover is less likely to be needed in the winter. These pack covers are a bother in any season, but they're about the only way to guarantee that your pack's contents will stay dry. Ponchos that have an extension will fit over the pack, but they are not recommended for winter travel; they snag on brush, catch wind like a spinnaker, and are seldom necessary if you wear a wind- and water-repellent parka and pants.

Zippers: Check zippers to be certain they work freely, and always keep them lubricated with paraffin or some other agent that is impervious to the cold. Nearly all pack zippers are made of plastic rather than metal because plastic won't freeze as easily. Most frozen zippers are caused by moisture that has collected in the tape rather than in the teeth. A bottle of silicone spray helps keep them clear.

BUYING A SLEEPING BAG

Sleeping bags come in two basic shapes: mummy and rectangular. Common variations of sleeping bags are simply modified versions of the basic mummy and rectangular styles.

For winter camping and backpacking, the most popular sleeping bags are the mummy configurations because they take up less space and are warmer and lighter.

The bags have built-in hoods with drawstrings. Some have a pocket in the hood that can be used to pack a sweater or down jacket for a pillow.

You have two choices of insulating material in a sleeping bag: goose down and synthetics. Goose down is the best insulation known because it is light and compact; it will last through generations of campers if treated properly.

The alternative to goose down is synthetic insulation. Synthetics continue to improve in quality and have several advantages; they are lower in cost, they can get wet and still retain their loft and insulating ability, and they can simply be wrung out when wet. The disadvantages of synthetics are that they weigh more than down, they wear out sooner, and they are bulkier when put into a stuff bag.

Loft—the thickness of the insulation—is an important quality of sleeping bags and some articles of clothing. The more loft, the more insulation value the bag or garment has. When a sleeping bag is put into a stuff bag, it has virtually no loft because loft depends on dead-air space for its effectiveness. But when the sleeping bag is removed and fluffed up, the insulation returns to its normal shape and you have loft again.

Synthetic insulation is available under many brand names, including Hollofil, PolarGuard, Fiberfill, Thinsulate, Fortrel, Kodel, and Quallofil. These synthetics are made of petroleum derivatives and come in individually curled pieces, batts, and other designs.

Sleeping bag shells are made of a variety of materials. Goose down-insulated bags must be made of strong and tightly woven fabrics to avoid

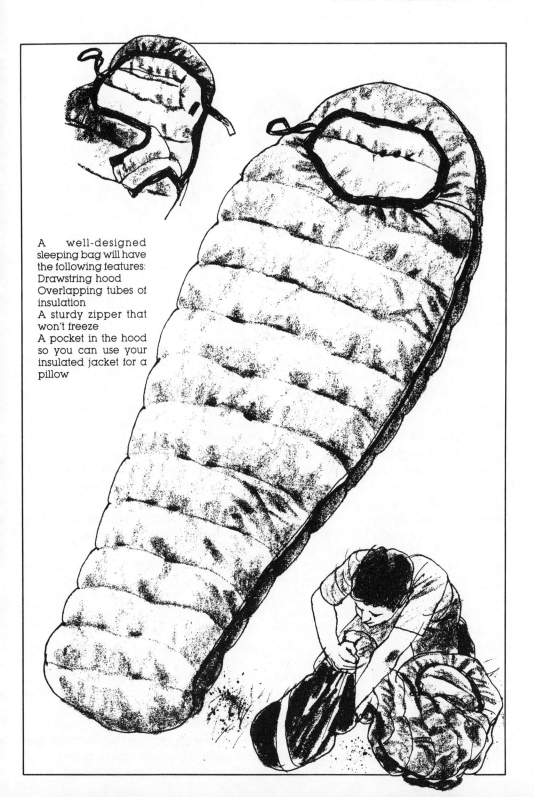

A well-designed sleeping bag will have the following features:
Drawstring hood
Overlapping tubes of insulation
A sturdy zipper that won't freeze
A pocket in the hood so you can use your insulated jacket for a pillow

The basic shapes of sleeping bags are, from left, the rectangular, the modified rectangular, a modified mummy, and a pure mummy bag. Most backpackers use the mummy shape because of weight and insulation factors.

leaking down out through the weave. For example, hi count taffeta, which is nylon, is used in many bags because it is down-proof. A popular material for the sleeping bag liner is Tri Blend, which contains polyester, cotton, and nylon; it provides the comfort of cotton next to your skin and also resists shrinkage.

A third material is Ramar, a rugged poplin blend of 60 percent cotton and 40 percent nylon. It is extremely resistant to tears and abrasions and combines the strength of nylon with the comfort of cotton.

When purchasing a sleeping bag for a specific use or season, consider the several methods of construction that are available. Most down bags feature "sewn-through" or "slant-box" construction. The sewn-through method is best for use in mild temperatures because the stitching leaves uninsulated areas that allow heat to escape. The slant-box method is better for cold weather because the interior walls are slanted to form baffles that overlap seams and down channels. The best bags use a stretch fabric in the sidewalls to accommodate the stretching and flexing of the body, eliminating

"cold spots" and keeping the down distributed evenly.

Common construction methods for synthetic insulation are "double offset quilt" and "sandwich." The double offset system has two quilted layers of insulation to maintain even lofting. This method is commonly used in mild-weather bags. The sandwich method places insulation between two layers of quilted material and attaches it at the edges to avoid shifting. This system is most often used in cold-weather synthetic bags.

Other factors to consider when choosing a sleeping bag include proper stitching, which should be eight to ten stitches per inch; differential cut, so that the outer shell is larger than the inner shell; side-block baffle (for goose-down bags), which is placed opposite the zipper side to keep the down form shifting; baffled foot section, which also keeps the down from shifting; and differential loft, which has about 60 percent of the insulation on top where the body weight won't compress it.

The best bags have sturdy zipper enclosures, Velcro fasteners, and drawcords that operate smoothly.

Hoods extend the comfort range of sleeping bags, as do liners that are tied in and provide more warmth. The best hoods also have a pillow pocket where you can stuff a sweater or jacket for more comfort.

All sleeping bags should be carried in a waterproof stuffbag.

METHODS OF DOWN CONSTRUCTION

Sewn-through

Slant-wall

Offset quilt

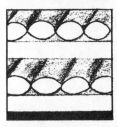

Double offset

CARE AND STORAGE

When you return from a trip, your sleeping bags should be aired out to allow any moisture to escape. Then store them loosely to allow the insulation and seams to relax. Do not store your bag in a stuffed manner for a long period of time, because it can cause the insulation to break down and places undue stress on the bag's construction.

Goose-down bags can be dry cleaned or hand-washed. If dry cleaned, choose a shop that is experienced in the care of goose-down products. A shop that does not have this experience can damage the down. Check with your outdoor equipment store for advice—Eddie Bauer stores keep a list of shops with experience in cleaning down.

If you decide to hand-wash your sleeping bag, use a bathtub because you will need the room. Fill the tub half full of lukewarm water and add Ivory Flakes or a mild liquid soap such as Woolite.

Submerge the bag in the water, pressing down until it is fully saturated. Gently scrub any soiled areas and let the bag soak for 12 hours, turning and rotating it occasionally to loosen dirt.

A word of caution: When saturated with water, your bag may weigh more than 100 pounds. Do not attempt to lift it, because you will damage the seams, stitching, or internal construction.

Drain the tub while pressing on the

bag to remove excess water. Then re-fill the tub with lukewarm water and turn the bag to rinse out the soap. Drain and refill the tub again. Repeat this process until the rinse water is free from soap.

Press and squeeze out as much water as possible; then gather the bag in your arms and place it in a large washing machine or a centrifuge water extractor. Distribute the bag evenly around the drum. Set the machine on "spin cycle," which will help extract the water from the bag.

After most of the water is removed, place the bag in a large commercial dryer with the thermostat set on "low heat." Put a clean tennis shoe in with the bag to help distribute the down evenly as the bag dries. Drying time will be from 6 to 24 hours.

TENTS

Even if you already own a tent for backpacking, chances are it is not suitable for winter camping, unless you had the foresight to buy one that can be adapted to winter use.

The standard tent for both summer and winter consists of these basic parts:

Fabric: A breathable, lightweight nylon, usually ripstop nylon, that draws the moisture from your body and breath through the walls and ceiling to prevent condensation buildup. The floor and about six inches of the side-wall should be waterproof. The tent should have fine-screen netting over all openings to keep bugs out; it may also have netting pockets sewn into the walls for storing flashlights and other small items.

The tent should be covered with a waterproof rainfly that stands a few inches away from the tent, which will ensure air circulation to take away the moisture. The rainfly comes out over the entrance of the tent to form a small porch.

The tent should be supported with a system of poles made of either aluminum or fiberglass; remember that aluminum is more lightweight. Most newer tents are free-standing, meaning that they don't need guy lines to stand. A free-standing tent has the tension built into the framework. Most tents also have tabs for stakes, if for no other reason than to keep the tent from blowing away.

When the basic tent is built and used properly, it is completely water-proof, does not allow condensation to collect on the interior walls, and can ride out a severe storm without collapsing or blowing away.

The best tents are also very light-weight. You can buy a good tent that weighs less than 10 pounds, poles and all, and will hold three adults and some of their gear. Most tents in this weight category have two carrying bags—one for the tent and the other for stakes, poles, and other accessories—so that tent mates can share the load.

Winter Adaptations: The same basic features found in summer tents are also found in winter designs, but with a few added features. Remember that backpacking tents aren't designed to keep you warm; they are made of a breathable fabric that not only lets moisture out but also lets cold air in. However, due to the rain fly, they do give protection against the wind, snow, and rain.

Some winter tents have these additional features:

Entrances: There are two main

Lightweight backpacker
tent with vestibule

types of entrances, the "tunnel" and the "vestibule." Both entrance types will help avoid frozen tent zippers.

The tunnel entrance is a large tube that extends away from the regular entrance. It is usually made of the same material as the tent walls. This tunnel enables you to get in and out of the tent without having snow blow in behind you; it also provides an addi-

tional storage place for packs and cooking equipment, which may be handy at night.

The tunnel entrance can even be detached from some tents and stored for the summer. Make sure that the tunnel portion can be rolled back around the regular entrance and tied out of the way with strings attached to the tent.

External frame
dome tent
with rain fly

Four-season tent with
rain fly and tunnel storm entry

Vestibule entrances are porches for tents that extend out over the entrance—they can be used for gear storage, as a cooking area, and to find protection from the wind and weather. Vestibules are also usually detachable for summer use.

Cookhole: A few winterized tents have a circular zipper in the center of the tent floor that allows you to put the camp stove on the snow or bare ground and avoid the danger of fire or damage from spilling food; this should be done only when you have no other choice. A cookhole prevents the floor of the tent from being waterproof because water can almost always seep through the seam. If you own a tent with cookhole, you must use a groundcloth between the tent and the ground (which is a good idea for **all** tents).

Frost liner: Many winter tents come equipped with inside loops across the top and around the sides to attach frost liners, which are very useful in cold

QUALITY IN TENTS

Consider these things when looking at a tent to be certain it is of high quality:

Catenary cut: This is a curved stiching design that is particularly important on A-frame tents; it runs across the ride line so that you can keep it taut. Straight seams in stress areas are more difficult to keep taut.

Vent: The rear of the tent should have a vent, usually a small tunnel with the end covered with nylon mesh that is fine enough to keep out bugs. The end should also have a drawstring so that you can close it off to keep out breezes.

Tunnel entrance: This is almost essential for winter camping because it gives you more flexibility in the size of the tent opening and prevents frozen zippers.

Nylon zippers: Metal zippers are notorious for freezing; nylon zippers won't freeze nor will they stick to your fingers when it is cold.

Pole pockets: If your tent has external poles that attach to the base of the tent (most free-standing tents have this feature), be certain the pole pockets are reinforced, preferably with nylon webbing.

Floor: The tent floor and the bottom few inches of the sidewalls should be waterproof, creating what some campers call a "tub floor."

Color: Most winter campers prefer warm colors for the tent and fly because of the psychological value gained in case you are forced to sit out bad weather for any extended period. The cold colors—greens and blues—are less popular than the warm colors—yellows, reds, and similar hues.

Hooks and Pockets: Cargo pockets or hooks on the inside of the tent are handy for hanging clothing or storing gear.

weather. Frost liners are usually cotton sheets that hang just below the top and walls of the tent; they collect the condensation in the air before it reaches the tent walls and freezes. Each morning the ice collected in the liner can be removed by shaking or gently beating the liner like a rug. A liner saves wear on the tent and also keeps the tent dry when it is stored in your pack.

Anchors: When you put up the tent, always use some kind of anchoring system, even if your tent is free-standing. Sometimes you can stamp the snow so it is firm enough to hold the skewer-type stakes that come with most tents, but it is best to find a more sufficient type of anchor. Use your skis, ski poles, ice axe, snowshoes, or special "deadman" snow anchors, except when you must leave the tent up all day while you ski in the area. In that case, don't depend on your transportation for anchors.

Some campers use Frisbees. They drill small holes in the plastic, attach the tent lines, and then bury them, packing the snow firmly over the Frisbee.

Size and shape: The size of your tent will depend on how many people are in your family or group and how cozy you all want to be. The three- or four-man models are probably the best size, even for only two persons, because there will be room to store your gear at night. Equipment left lying outside in the snow overnight has a way of disappearing. The only safe place for it is in the tent, away from falling or drifting snow.

Tent shape should follow the same theory that the Swiss have always used in building houses with steep roofs: The sharper the pitch, the less snow that

will build up. It doesn't take much wet snow to collapse a tent on its occupants, bending or breaking the poles and ruining the entire trip. Pyramid, dome, and steep A-frame designs are best for snow. No matter how steep the tent is, if you're caught in a snowstorm, keep a lookout for the telltale downward bulge of the ceiling and walls and keep the stakes and lines in place.

DRESSING FOR WINTER CAMPING

We have already discussed what the properly dressed x-c skier should wear when he uses the layering system. We have planned for active day-long outings with no allowances made for skiing in foul weather or on overnight trips away from central heating systems and electric blankets.

Now we will discuss clothing all over again, because what you need for short day outings is not adequate for longer camping trips. On a camping trip you exercise strenuously and are then relatively inactive for several hours at a time. You will also be outdoors during the coldest part of the day, those early-morning hours between midnight and dawn when the temperature takes its most dramatic drop.

First Layer: Wear fishnet **underwear** that traps body heat in dead-air space between your skin and the next layer of clothing. Or try a two-layer union suit; Duofold is a common brand. The layer next to your skin is made of cotton to wick away the moisture; an insulating air space fills in between the cotton and the outer layer, which is wool or a wool-and-nylon blend.

Layer-dressing for an
overnight x-c trip

Silk or light polyester **socks** should be worn against the skin for comfort and to wick away moisture to the outer layer.

Second Layer: Your next layer of clothing depends on what you are wearing for boots and how cold it is.

With **ski-boots** wear a second pair of heavy wool, calf-length socks.

With **shoe pacs** wear either felt liners (with a spare pair to always have one dry pair) or quilted synthetic liners, such as those made of PolarGuard or Thinsulate. You may need to wear these pacs if you are going to be in rugged country where you have to alternate skiing with snowshoeing. In this case, you will need special bindings that are adjustable to a variety of boot types.

For **pants**, depending on the tem-perature, you can wear a pair of heavy, densely woven wool pants or an intermediate layer of pants, such as quilted goose down or polyester.

For a **shirt**, wear a heavy wool shirt, or if very cold, a quilted lightweight goose-down or polyester shirt, to match the extra pair of pants.

Outer Layer: Your **boots**, as already noted, will depend on the weather and the form of transportation. If you are going to ski as well as snowshoe, you'll need special bindings on the skis. A variety of pacs are offered, ranging from ankle-length to the high tops that go over the calf, negating the need for gaiters. However, most skiers prefer lower-cut models for freedom of movement, with a pair of gaiters to cover the leg from ankle to calf. Another alternative for pac liners

is a Finnish product called **tossus**, which is made of raw wool that is shaped by hand around the foot. They are said to retain their shape and fluffiness under repeated and rugged use.

All winter clothing is important, but footwear is perhaps the most important. The feet are farthest from the heart and the most difficult extremity to keep warm or to warm up after they get cold. Hands can be tucked under an armpit to rewarm. Ears and nose can be rewarmed with hands. But cold feet are a different matter. Thus, take no chances on getting the proper footgear.

The best **pants** are usually lightweight, water-repellent windpants. They should be cut loosely for freedom of movement and to allow for a variety of pants beneath. The legs can

be tucked into boots or gaiters. The pants can be held up either by belt or suspenders. Many outdoorsmen choose what has become known as snowmobilers' pants, which are insulated with either down or a synthetic and covered with a water- and wind-resistant nylon.

A good **shirt** combination is a two-part system consisting of a wool shirt and a wool sweater. The shirt is usually warm enough for trail wear, but when you stop for lunch or overnight, you'll need the additional warmth of a wool sweater beneath the parka. Pullovers, either crew or turtleneck, are the most popular, but some find button sweaters (cardigans) enough.

The **parka** is the other half of a matching set of wind-proof and water-repellent outer gear. The parka should

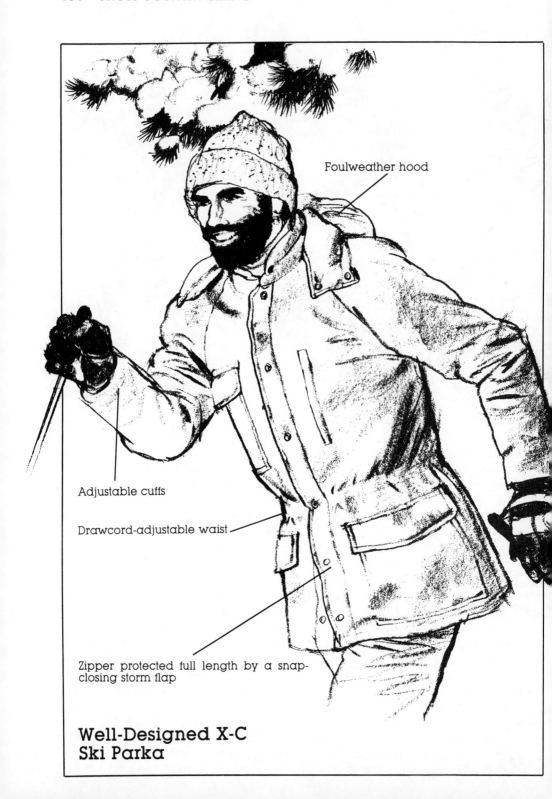

Foulweather hood

Adjustable cuffs

Drawcord-adjustable waist

Zipper protected full length by a snap-closing storm flap

Well-Designed X-C Ski Parka

be loosely cut, should have a hood with drawstring and some method of closing the cuffs to keep cold air out or to let it in for ventilation. The longer parkas also have a waist drawstring to alternately trap dead air for warmth or to let it escape for ventilation. Some are lined with nylon or wool, some are not.

For your **hands**, insulated ski gloves are preferred by most people because freedom of movement is needed for skiing and camping. They are sufficient for most conditions. Add a pair of nylon liners and they are good for temperatures down to freezing or even lower.

But the best and safest handwear are mittens. Good mittens, which aren't always easy to find, are the kind made for soldiers and airmen with a thumb and index finger. This makes it possible for you to perform some functions without taking them off.

Your mittens should have an outer shell of poplin or Gore-Tex and should be long enough to come well over the cuffs of the parka. The inside liner should be of wool for warmth. Always carry two pairs of liners so one can be hung out to dry or tucked into the sleeping bag with you overnight to dry.

Some people wear a pair of soft leather gloves with the mitten liners and shell over them. This permits them to take off the mittens to make minor repairs, light a match or whatever, without freezing fingers or having to touch a metal object with bare fingers.

On your **head** you should wear either a wool watchcap that can be rolled down over your ears or rolled up when your head is too warm. You wear this cap beneath the hood of the wind parka. In extreme temperatures, a watchcap with facemask can be

---

SKI TIP

The pockets on your parka might ruin the streamlined look you prefer, but the more pockets you have, the more safety items you can carry, such as: matches, trail food, compass, water bottles, extra articles of clothing, sunscreen, a whistle, and even litter found along the trail.

---

worn that covers everything except your eyes and nose and is long enough to tuck into the top of your shirt.

The best facemasks are made of nylon and insulated with goose down. These have eye holes; but instead of simply a hole for your nose, they have a down-insulated beak that covers all of your nose except the nostrils.

ADDITIONAL CLOTHING

Since you will be traveling light, either carrying everything in a pack

---

SKI TIP

The best type of parka has a drawstring at the waist that you can adjust to increase or decrease ventilation. Some also have a drawstring at the bottom to keep the parka snug around your hips, which is handy for keeping out the snow when you fall.

HEADGEAR

Various kinds of headgear for winter travel **A**—Wool watch cap. **B**—Billed cap with ear flaps. **C**—Goose down insultated face mask. **D**—Balaclava cap with bill. **E**—Balaclava with knit cap over it.

or towing it along behind in a **pulka**, additional clothing will be as lightweight and compact as possible. In spite of great improvements made in synthetic insulating material, nothing has yet been found to produce the most efficient insulation at a lesser weight and bulk than goose down. Some synthetics are coming closer, but there remains at least a 10 percent difference in both bulk and weight between goose down and its synthetic imitators.

However, synthetics have the advantage in one major area: When they get wet, they can be wrung out to dry and they do not lose their loft when wet. Wet down dries very slowly, cannot be wrung out, and has no insulative value.

For winter travel, though, down is still superior, in part because the risk of getting wet in the winter is less than in the summer. Precipitation will be snow and not rain. You won't perspire

SKI TIP

You'll never have too many matches while camping in the snow. Carry your matches in the waterproof containers you use for summer camping, but keep other matches in your pockets, your stove, and tucked away where they'll always be handy.

As a backup, take at least one disposable cigarette lighter; use it only for camping purposes, so you'll always be sure it has fuel. Also take along chemical firestarter pellets or tubes. Remember, fire is your best friend in the winter.

SURVIVAL KITS

Most recreational stores stock survival kits that come in a container no larger than a pipe-tobacco can. More elaborate and expensive kits are available and make good gifts for campers in all seasons. The typical kit contains these items:

- Tube tent
- Whistle
- Candle
- Matches
- Duct tape
- Aluminum foil
- Energy candy bars
- Bouillon cubes
- Signal mirror
- First-aid supplies
- Fire starter
- Nylon cord
- Razor blade
- Dextrose cubes
- Herb tea bags
- Waterproof survival instructions

All of these items will pack into a surprisingly small container for use in emergency situations. If nothing else, reading the kit's instructions and examining its contents while brewing a pot of tea will keep your mind off your present problem long enough for you to calm down and think clearly. But· emergency provisions and kits will do you no good if you leave them behind because they make an unsightly lump in your ski clothing or because you will be gone just "a little while."

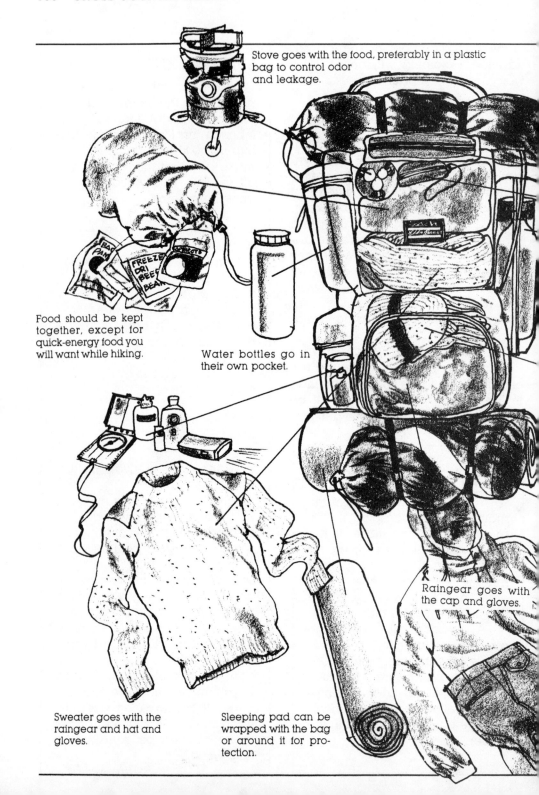

Stove goes with the food, preferably in a plastic bag to control odor and leakage.

Food should be kept together, except for quick-energy food you will want while hiking.

Water bottles go in their own pocket.

Sweater goes with the raingear and hat and gloves.

Sleeping pad can be wrapped with the bag or around it for protection.

Raingear goes with the cap and gloves.

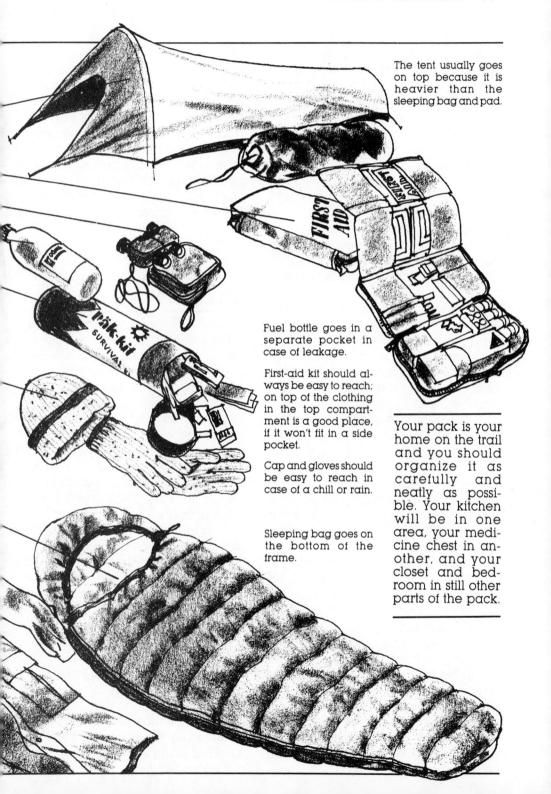

The tent usually goes on top because it is heavier than the sleeping bag and pad.

Fuel bottle goes in a separate pocket in case of leakage.

First-aid kit should always be easy to reach; on top of the clothing in the top compartment is a good place, if it won't fit in a side pocket.

Cap and gloves should be easy to reach in case of a chill or rain.

Sleeping bag goes on the bottom of the frame.

Your pack is your home on the trail and you should organize it as carefully and neatly as possible. Your kitchen will be in one area, your medicine chest in another, and your closet and bedroom in still other parts of the pack.

nearly as much in the winter, and in the case of sleeping bags, snow is much easier to remove from a tent than summer moisture. Condensation that gathers on the tent walls in the summer and drips down on your sleeping bag and parka will turn into frost or ice during the winter. If your tent is equipped with a frost liner, the liner can be taken outside each morning and the ice crystals shaken off.

The best down-filled parkas for winter camping are those which can be worn under your wind parka during lunch or in the evening, then stuffed into a carrying bag when traveling. Many newer models are simply stuffed into one of the pockets rather than a separate bag.

Your parka should have a goose down-insulated hood, either permanently attached to the parka or easily attached with zipper or snaps.

By adding a goose down-insulated parka to your layering system, perhaps substituting it for the wool sweater, the difference in comfort range is enormous. For example, a parka that is rated to 0° F can be good for as much as 40° F more when worn with the fishnet or two-layer underwear, a wool shirt, and wind parka.

Under most circumstances you won't need additional insulated pants to match the goose down-insulated parka because the legs above your boots don't tend to get as cold as your trunk, where the vital organs are. Generally, if the trunk is warm, the blood circulates freely enough in the legs to keep them warm, provided the feet are well-insulated.

Another item to consider for camp use is a pair of goose-down booties, so you can take off your boots and remove the liners to be dried. These will not only give your boots and liners a rest; they also will give your feet a rest. They are excellent for wearing in the sleeping bag, provided they are totally dry. Some campers carry two pairs of these booties, one the heavy-duty type with the attached soles, and another pair which are little more than down-filled socks to wear to bed. Both types weigh only ounces and can be compressed to take up very little space.

THE WINTER KITCHEN

Since the point of going camping in the winter is to enjoy the outdoors, you won't be interested in devoting any more time to cooking than absolutely necessary So keep it simple, keep it nutritious, and keep it warm. Of course, if gourmet cooking is one of your hobbies, and you wouldn't think of going into the wilderness without taking along a few touches of elegance, fine. But for most campers, simplicity and nutrition are primary considerations.

Actually, cooking and eating on a winter trip are usually more enjoyable than eating during the summer when you have to battle mosquitoes, flies, gnats, moths, and several species of rodents who hang around the camp like maurading bands of desert thieves. You don't have to worry so much about food spoiling, so you can indulge your love of fruits and vegetables, and you can store perishables in sealed containers hanging from tree branches or hidden in the snow with a pole or string attached so you won't lose them.

This brings up an aside worth mentioning while you're thinking about knives, can openers, jar lids, and other small items. There's an old adage that "snow is the biggest thief in the North," meaning that things have a way of getting lost in the snow. One minute it is lying on top of a snowbank; the next it is gone, perhaps several feet down into the drift. Other campers blame it on the **maymaygushies**, a mythical little creature invented by winter travelers who keep losing things. They also accuse snow of "eating" things.

Whatever you decide to call it, you should build a kitchen area on a flat and stamped-out surface with something between the utensils and the snow, such as a piece of tarp, a board, a flattened cardboard box—anything that will keep the snow bandits from stealing your utensils.

If your snow is deep enough, you can build elaborate systems of shelves, seating platforms, and so on, by digging down into a drift and stamping the snow flat around the sides. This gives your camp a sand-castle effect because you can use the area while you're there, then let the snow, sun, and spring demolish it with no traces. No environmental impact statements are required for this kind of wilderness construction.

UTENSILS

Again, keep it simple. A set of nesting pots, no more than three, with a stove that fits inside, a cup and plate, tableware, stirring spoon, potlifter or vice grips—and that is about all you'll need. Of course, if you insist on pancakes, real bacon and eggs, biscuits, and other unnecessary but tasty dishes, you won't be satisfied with such a spartan kitchen.

You should try to avoid metal utensils, plates, cups, and dishes because they not only can cause you to freeze your fingers or lips and tongue when you touch them, they also conduct heat too well and can cause burns on numb fingers and lips. Plastic is much better for winter use.

BASIC FOODS

Since you will be treating food more as fuel than as an intellectual or sensual experience, you will want to keep each meal simple and basic. The cook isn't going to be anxious to fuss over an omelette when the temperature is below freezing, particularly if you are the cook.

Breakfast can be no more than coffee, hot chocolate, or tea, a bowl of crunchy granola with reconstituted milk, and perhaps dried fruit. You may want to keep the stove going under a pot of water so you can load a thermos with hot soup or hot chocolate for lunch.

Lunch can be trail food—dried fruit, chocolate bar, gorp (good old raisins and peanuts), cheese, or a can of meat spread for the pilot bread. Since spoilage isn't a major problem, a few slices of bread and lunchmeat will be welcome. You can fire up a stove for a hot drink or to make a cup of soup from a ready-mix.

Dinner should be a one-pot meal: beef stroganoff, macaroni and cheese with a shredded bacon bar or meat bar sprinkled on it, followed by an instant dessert such as pudding or granola bars.

It is important to remember that you will need more food for winter camping than summer. Your system

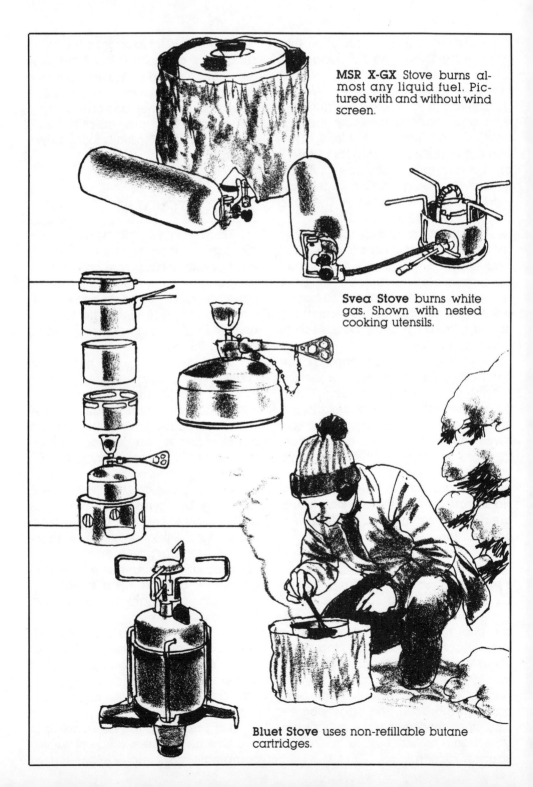

MSR X-GX Stove burns almost any liquid fuel. Pictured with and without wind screen.

Svea Stove burns white gas. Shown with nested cooking utensils.

Bluet Stove uses non-refillable butane cartridges.

will be consuming more food to keep the body furnace warm and ward off the cold. Also, x-c skiing is strenuous. This, combined with the need to stay warm, amounts to more food than usual.

Within this nutritional framework

As a general rule, you should figure on about two and a half pounds of food per person per day; this is dry weight, not including the amount of water required to reconstitute dehydrated or freeze-dried foods. To yield at least 4,500 calories per day, which is the minimum daily requirement for adults in cold weather, you should plan your menus according to the following nutrient and weight breakdown:

Nutrient	Pounds
Fats	.25
Starches	.9
Sugars	.4
Protein	.6
Beverages	.1

Fats: Butter, peanut butter, meat bars, nuts, oil

Starches: Cereals, noodles, rice, potatoes, bread, soups, freeze-dried vegetables

Sugars: White or dark sugar, candy, pudding, honey, dried fruits

Protein: Meats, cheeses, milk, eggs

Beverages: Coffee, tea, chocolate mixes, fruit mixes

---

you can draw up a menu for any length of trip with a great variety of foods, and you can always remove the blandness from the dishes by adding spices. Curry powder does wonders to a bland macaroni and cheese dinner. A cinnamon stick will turn a cup of hot chocolate into a genuine treat. Stretch your imagination a bit and you will be surprised at how tasty an ordinary dish can become.

And remember: Nights are long during the winter and the dinner hour can be stretched simply to fill the time between darkness and bedtime. So unless your kitchen is away from the tents, you can eat three or four leisurely courses between performing the other camp chores before bedtime.

STOVES

Some popular stoves are those that nest into the cooking pots, and the best of all are those with pumps. The worst of all for cold-weather use—because they probably won't work at all—are those that burn butane and propane. Butane stoves, a favorite for summer use because they are so simple to use, are useless in winter because they don't work below freezing; the fuel freezes at 15° F. Propane will still vaporize in freezing temperatures but is pressurized in a heavy steel cartridge that grows heavier by the step.

Consequently, the white gas or alcohol stoves equipped with a pressure pump are the best. Some models must be primed to heat up the vaporizing tube between the tank and burner. The usual way to do this is to place a small amount of fuel or alcohol on the burner, then ignite it and let it burn for a few minutes. When the whole burner mechanism is hot, the valve is turned on to let the fuel enter the vaporizing tube and become vapor instead of liquid.

The problem with this, of course, is that if the temperature is very low, the preheating might take much longer than normal. Danger is built into this system, especially inside a tent, because the fuel can be accidentally spilled and your stove will become a torch in the tent. However, if the cooking is done outside or always inside the vestibule, that danger is lessened.

Always carry a cleaning wire if your stove does not have one built in, more than one in case you lose one in the snow, and spare parts, such as those small plates that sit on top of burners and fall off at regular intervals.

Fuel containers should be sturdy plastic or aluminum, and be sure you carry enough for your trip. Your summer fuel needs will almost double during winter outings because it takes longer to cook in the cold. In addition, you'll probably use the stove more for hot drinks throughout the evening. (See equipment lists for estimated fuel use.)

SKI TIP

A can of silicone spray will help keep the mohair strips on the bottom of your skis from icing up. If your skis do ice up, try dipping them in water until the ice loosens; then stride across the snow without lifting the skis so the snow will absorb the water.

TEN ESSENTIALS

This list of "Ten Essentials," which is now one of the standard expressions in all sports and all seasons, should be followed quite carefully, particularly if you plan to ski from a base camp or lodge and away from immediate help.

Extra Food: Always keep the equivalent of a day's supply of food for each person in your group. Freeze-dried or dehydrated foods are good choices because they are lightweight and compact.

Extra Clothing: Even though you'll dress according to the layering system, you should bring along dry clothing with you, including a change of socks, pants, and shirt, in case you overexert or get wet in some other fashion. Store this extra set of clothing in a waterproof plastic bag.

Matches in Waterproof Container: Keep a container filled and carry it in a pocket in addition to the other camp matches.

Candle or Firestarter: Keep a few stubs of household candles scattered throughout the camping equipment, as well as one in your pocket; they are always needed for starting fires with wet wood. An even better solution is to carry a tube or can of chemical firestarting pellets and reserve it for emergency use only. Then you'll have the candles for light and firestarter for fires.

First-Aid Kit: This should in-

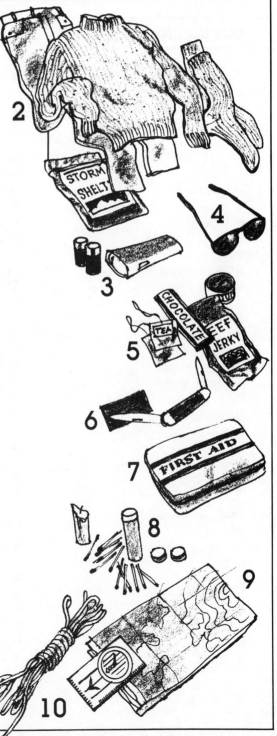

clude the following: Band Aids for small cuts, gauze pads of various sizes, adhesive tape, salt tablets, aspirin, a needle for blisters, and a first-aid manual. Also pack moleskin for covering blisters, a single-edge razor blade, Halazone tablets for purifying water or a chemical drinking straw, first-aid cream, a mild antiseptic such as Bactine, antihistamine tablets for allergies, sunscreen, and lip salve. Also be sure to bring along any prescription drugs you may have to take.

Maps: Carry topographical maps of the areas you will be touring. Study them before leaving home to make sure you know how to use them.

Compass: Carry one at all times—know how to use it, too.

Flashlight, Spare Batteries, and Bulb: Always keep one set of batteries tucked away and sealed.

Knife and Sharpening Tool: The best belt knives have short blades; the best pocket knives are similar to the old Boy Scout knife that has a big blade, a can opener, an awl, and a screwdriver. The Swiss Army knives are fine, too, but if your fingers are cold or the weather is cool enough to cause freezing, you'll curse your 24-blade knife.

Sunglasses: These are a definite must for winter camping. Attach an elastic holder to keep them from falling off.

EQUIPMENT CHECKLIST

Clothing—Inner Layer
- Long johns, top and bottom
- Inner socks
- Liner gloves or mittens
- Vapor barrier (if you prefer plastic bags for socks)

Insulating Layer
- Down or fiberfill parka
- Wool shirt
- Wool sweater
- Turtleneck
- Wool pants or knickers
- Wool socks

Protective Layer
- Windshirt or parka with hood
- Rainjacket
- Windpants
- Mitten shells

Other Clothing
- Suspenders or belt
- Bandana
- Facemask or balaclava hat
- Gaiters

Feet
- Ski boots
- Felt or synthetic insoles
- Extra socks
- Insulated booties
- Overboots

Camp Kitchen
- Stove
- Fuel bottles
- Matches in waterproof container
- Funnel (if fuel bottle doesn't have spout)
- Fuel pellets
- Nesting cookware
- Pot gripper
- Plastic cups
- Eating utensils
- Food
- Small square of ensolite to put under stove

Emergency Kit
- Spare matches in waterproof container
- Fuel pellets or firestarter
- Compass
- Knife
- Whistle
- Coins for phone calls
- Package of nylon clothesline cord
- Spare food
- Signal mirror
- Avalanche beacon or avalanche cord

Repair Kit
- Needle
- Nylon thread or dental floss
- Duct tape
- Thin sheet metal to repair poles
- Epoxy
- Screwdriver to fit ski heads
- Vice grips
- Spare binding screws

- Spare ski tip
- Pack repair items (clevis pins, etc.)
- Spare cables for cable binding
- Small roll of bailing wire or picture wire
- Extra pole basket or different type
- Spare stove parts
- Stove cleaning wire

First-Aid Kit

- Roll of moleskin
- Two or three triangular bandages
- Six sterile pads
- Anti-acid tablets
- Ace bandages
- Assorted Band Aids
- Selection of butterfly bandages
- Aspirin
- Prescription medicine
- Sunglasses
- First-aid tape
- Four-inch tape
- Sunburn cream
- Chapstick
- First-aid book

Wax Kit

- Waxes
- Scraper
- Cork
- Wax remover
- Rag
- Hand cleaner

Miscellaneous

- Snow saw
- Headlamp and flashlight
- Extra candles
- Watch
- Notepaper and pencil
- Reading material
- Thermometer
- Games
- Sunburn lotion
- Toilet gear

Personal Equipment

- Skis and bindings
- Poles
- Skins or rope climbers
- Sleeping bag
- Sleeping pad
- Tent
- Candle lantern
- Snowshoes

Group Items

- Shovel (one for every two persons)

PART V
WHERE TO GO

CHAPTER 13

RESOURCES

PUBLICATIONS

The growth of cross-country skiing has been almost explosive during the past decade. The National Ski Touring Operators Association lists at least 600 touring centers throughout North America; perhaps another 100 to 200 exist but have not yet joined the association. For a list of all the ski areas in North America, write for:

White Book of Ski Areas
  380 Madison Avenue
  New York, NY 10017

In addition to the sources listed in the acknowledgments, here's a list of consumer publications with material about x-c skiing:

SKI Magazine
  380 Madison Avenue
  New York, NY 10017
Skiing Magazine
  One Park Avenue
  New York, NY 10016
Powder Magazine
  Box 1028
  Dana Point, CA 92629
Ski Racing
  Box 70
  Fair Haven, VT 05743
Ski America
  370 Wahconah Street
  Pittsfield, MA 01201

Skier's World
  1400 Stierlin Road
  Mountain View, CA 94042
United States Ski News
  P.O. Box 100
  Park City, UT 84060

ASSOCIATIONS

The United States Ski Association has regional chapters throughout America and both national and regional committees on various aspects of x-c skiing. You can obtain information on these subjects by writing the headquarters:

USSA
  Box 100
  Park City, UT 84060

Another source is:

Ski Touring Council
  Troy, VT 05868

For information on Canadian skiing, including nearly every aspect of the sport, from coaching to racing, write:

Canadian Ski Association
  333 River Road
  Ottawa, Ontario
  K1L 8B9, Canada

INDEX